365 Names of God
YOUTH CURRICULUM

John Paul Jackson
and Jordan Bateman

INCLUDES TEACHER'S GUIDE AND STUDENT MATERIALS

STREAMS
PUBLISHING HOUSE
North Sutton, New Hampshire

I AM: 365 Names of God Youth Curriculum
Copyright © 2005 by John Paul Jackson

Requests for information should be addressed to:
Streams Publishing House
P.O. Box 550
North Sutton, New Hampshire 03260
1.888.441.8080
Website: http://www.streamsministries.com

Unless otherwise indicated, all Scripture quotations are taken from *The Holy Bible, New King James Version.* Copyright © 1979, 1980, 1982 by Thomas Nelson, Inc.

ISBN: 1-58483-093-X

Creative Director and Managing Editor: Carolyn Blunk
Assistant Editor: Mary Ballotte
Copy Editor: Dorian Kreindler
Editorial Assistant: Leslie Herrier
Designed by Kelly Noffsinger

Printed in the United States of America

FOR A FREE CATALOG OF STREAMS BOOKS AND OTHER MATERIALS, CALL 1.888.441.8080 (USA AND CANADA)

We dedicate this book to the parents,
youth pastors, workers, teachers,
coaches, mentors, and others who every day
give freely of themselves to shape the next generation.
We hope this resource helps you in your quest
to make those you have been entrusted with
more like Jesus.

"Great is the Lord, and greatly to be praised;
And His greatness is unsearchable.
One generation shall praise Your works to another,
And shall declare Your mighty acts.

My mouth shall speak the praise of the Lord,
And all flesh shall bless His holy name
Forever and ever."
Psalm 145:3–4, 21

OTHER BOOKS BY JOHN PAUL JACKSON

Breaking Free of Rejection

I AM: Inheriting the Fullness of God's Names

I AM: 365 Names of God

Moments with God Dream Journal

Unmasking the Jezebel Spirit

Buying and Selling the Souls of Our Children

Needless Casualties of War

CONTENTS

ACKNOWLEDGMENTS

Many individuals and groups graciously helped us shape this youth leader's resource. To them, we are greatly indebted.

Our families are always a blessing in every project we tackle. John Paul's wife, Diane, and son Micah, and Jordan's wife, Jenny, and baby daughter, Indiana, are true gifts.

This curriculum was field-tested in two Canadian churches. We would like to thank Jesse Padgett, Shabbir Bell, and Jennifer Bateman for teaching the curriculum at Friends Langley Vineyard's Bliss youth group. As well, we would like to thank Chad Eddy and Fort Richmond Baptist Church's Shine youth movement in Winnipeg, Canada, for their invaluable feedback. Your help made this material much stronger.

The amazing team at Streams Ministries, including Greg Mapes and Carolyn Blunk, were a huge support and encouragement in the process of putting this curriculum together. Their vision, passion, and love for God continually inspire us. We would also like to thank Ernie Freeman, Academic Dean of the Streams Institute for Spiritual Development, who reviewed the curriculum. A big thank you also goes to Dorian Kreindler who provided copy-editing assistance; and to Mary Ballotte, Pat and Paul Leary, Don Archibald, Liz McGee, and Roxanne Stewart who spotted proofreading errors. Finally, we are grateful to graphic designer Kelly Noffsinger for bringing the type and illustrations to life.

PREFACE

As a reference for your students' study of God's name, we have included the list of 365 names and attributes of God, each compiled in *I AM: 365 Names of God*. This book divides God's names into twelve categories and is a wonderful devotional tool. Each I AM comes with the Bible verse where God's name or attribute can be found. (You can order the book from Streams Ministries www.streamsministries.com or by calling toll-free 1.888.441.8080.)

GOD OF WONDERS

I AM the God who shows wonders.
I AM the Lord, and My voice is powerful and full of majesty.
I AM God; nothing is too hard for Me.
I AM God, who made all My wonderful works to be remembered.
I AM God, and My glory thunders.
I AM the Spirit of knowledge and understanding.
I AM the Holy Spirit that moved upon the deep.
I AM worthy of worship, glorious and incomparable.
I AM God, who makes Himself known through visions.
I AM *dunamis* power.
I AM the giver of all revelation.
I AM glorious and full of weighty splendor.
I AM He who ascended to the Father.
I AM the Triune God of Israel.
I AM God, who performs signs.
I AM God, who speaks in night seasons.
I AM the King of glory.
I AM He who searches the mind and heart.
I AM great and greatly to be praised.
I AM Yah and Yahweh.
I AM the Creator of all true worship.
I AM wisdom.
I AM omniscient.
I AM the Lord, who stretches out the Heavens.
I AM God who speaks.
I AM Jehovah Rapha, your healer.
I AM God, who declares new things before they spring forth.
I AM the answer of your tongue.
I AM prophecy fulfilled; never early, never late.
I AM God, who gives you dreams.
I AM above all who are thought to be gods.

GOD OF JUSTICE

I AM the righteous judge of all creation.
I AM the King of Kings.
I AM with the generation of the righteous.
I AM God; My statutes rejoice the heart.
I AM the One who makes unbreakable covenants with humanity.
I AM holy, pure, and undefiled.
I AM God; besides Me there is no god.
I AM God by whose standard all actions are weighed.

I AM God; My testimony is sure.
I AM God; My commandments enlighten the eyes.
I AM the witness on your behalf.
I AM righteous; kings humble themselves before Me.
I AM God, whose eyelids test the sons of men.
I AM the Spirit of wisdom.
I AM My ordinances.
I AM the divine judge of all things.
I AM the law.
I AM my statutes; walk in them.
I AM judge of the living and the dead.
I AM the Spirit of the fear of the Lord.
I AM righteous.
I AM perfect knowledge.
I AM before whom every tongue will confess.
I AM the Lord, who loves righteousness.
I AM the unbiased, impartial judge.
I AM the Lord, and My judgments are righteous altogether.
I AM He who sent Moses to deliver Israel.
I AM God, and no one can reverse My acts.
I AM to be feared above all gods.
I AM God, who refines you.
I AM My judgments.
I AM the Lord who heals you.

 GOD OF SYMBOLS
I AM found in My appointed feasts.
I AM the anointing oil.
I AM the bright cloud that comes to you.
I AM the synagogue, church, tabernacle, and temple.
I AM the living water of life.
I AM the shofar-trumpet.
I AM the fountain of Israel.
I AM Israel's living star.
I AM the Passover.
I AM the Ark of the Covenant.
I AM the Door.
I AM the altar of the tabernacle.
I AM the balm of Gilead.
I AM the rose of Sharon.
I AM the tree of life.
I AM the God of Bethel.
I AM the lily of the valley.
I AM God, whose Sabbaths are a sign between you and Me.
I AM the rainbow's color.
I AM the Rock; there is no other.
I AM the glory in the cloud of the temple.
I AM the bread of life.
I AM your Rock, full of living water.
I AM the light of the world.
I AM a consuming fire.

I AM the north, your promoter.
I AM the Bright and Morning Star.
I AM the light, luminous, glowing, and radiant One.

GOD OF PROMISE
I AM returning.
I AM God, and I want you to believe in Me.
I AM He who places your tears in My bottle, in My book.
I AM God, who shows you things to come.
I AM the seven Spirits, and they are Me.
I AM the Lord; the fear of Me is a fountain of life.
I AM God; My secrets are with those who fear Me.
I AM life's guarantor of joy and health.
I AM God, who will be found by those who seek Me with all their heart and soul.
I AM, and you shall know My names.
I AM He who leads you in the paths of righteousness.
I AM the architect of the last days.
I AM the sole key giver of Heaven.
I AM the God who hears.
I AM the Lord who hears those who speak about My name.
I AM God, who leads you to prophesy.
I AM the soon-coming King.
I AM the Lord; I do not change.
I AM always with you, wherever you are.
I AM God, who speaks through dreams.
I AM God, who reveals His form.
I AM the healing you seek.
I AM the Savior, who will descend on the Mount of Olives.
I AM God, who gives you visions.
I AM God of those who are growing old.
I AM coming quickly.
I AM the One coming on the white horse.
I AM the soon-rending of the Heavens.
I AM the precision of My Scripture.
I AM waiting for you.

GOD THE SHEPHERD
I AM your shepherd; you shall not want.
I AM the rod that chastises and brings you comfort.
I AM in the desert wilderness to be tender with you.
I AM near to those who have a broken heart.
I AM your confidence.
I AM compassion.
I AM in the Father.
I AM with you and will keep you wherever you go.
I AM the refuge of the poor.
I AM your Father.
I AM God in the stillness.
I AM the Lord; he who is joined with Me is one spirit with Me.
I AM the Spirit of counsel.

I AM your provider.
I AM tenderness.
I AM the true shepherd.
I AM the dispeller of all fear and doubt.
I AM interceding for you right now.
I AM love.
I AM the staff that retrieves you.
I AM your friend, who sticks closer than a brother.
I AM the shepherd's rod.
I AM God, who is with you in the valley of the shadow of death.
I AM there with you.
I AM God, who strengthens you.
I AM the candle lighting your path.
I AM the Lord; precious in My sight is the death of all My saints.
I AM the Counselor, Mighty God, Everlasting Father.
I AM your peace and calm.
I AM He who wipes away your tears.
I AM the saving refuge of My anointed.

 GOD OF ETERNITY
I AM; I never change.
I AM the first and the last.
I AM one.
I AM humanity's builder of faith throughout the ages.
I AM ruler of both the night and the day.
I AM the uncaused, eternal, self-existent One.
I AM King forever and ever.
I AM Spirit.
I AM the Alpha and the Omega.
I AM God, whose eyes behold.
I AM the same every day.
I AM the Word of Life, called the Bible.
I AM the cornerstone.
I AM the resurrection and the life.
I AM not of this world.
I AM God, who knows all My works through eternity.
I AM omnipresent.
I AM the One who simultaneously sees beginning and end.
I AM God, ready to perform My word.
I AM three-in-one, equal and eternal.
I AM before the day was.
I AM all My names.
I AM the self-sufficient, self-sustaining, self-creating One.
I AM God; there is no other.
I AM the Word, which was in the beginning.
I AM the Rock of Ages on which you stand.
I AM He who was, and is, and is to come.
I AM Who I Am.
I AM the everlasting God.
I AM He who inhabits eternity.

GOD OF SACRIFICE
I AM the Christ.
I AM the cup of the blood.
I AM the eternal sacrifice.
I AM the blood that cleanses you from sin.
I AM the crucified Messiah of Calvary.
I AM your righteousness.
I AM the Yom Kippur offering to expiate all sins.
I AM worthy to open and read the scroll.
I AM Noah's Ark in a world still filled with sin.
I AM the wine and the bread.
I AM alive forevermore.
I AM the sprinkled blood of the Lamb on the doorposts of Israel.
I AM the Door to the Father.
I AM the Lord, who rescues those with a contrite spirit.
I AM God's Son, sent to be seen face-to-face.
I AM He who left Heaven for you.
I AM your sanctification.
I AM the blood atonement.
I AM God's only Son.
I AM eternally blind to what I've forgiven.
I AM the bread of life, broken for you.
I AM He who blots out your transgressions.
I AM supplication.
I AM the pierced Messiah.
I AM the Keeper of the keys to Hades and death.
I AM the God of your salvation.
I AM the Lamb that was slain.
I AM Father, Son, and Holy Spirit.
I AM outside the camp; come to Me.
I AM the way, the truth, and the life.

 GOD THE REWARD
I AM your exceedingly great reward.
I AM the Lord; taste and see that I am good.
I AM both the giver and the gifts.
I AM the preparer of your place in Heaven.
I AM able to give you much more than this.
I AM the one source of all true wealth.
I AM the Spirit of liberty.
I AM He who anoints your head with oil.
I AM the Bridegroom returning for My bride.
I AM the Lord, who looks on those who tremble at My Word.
I AM God, who prepares a table for you in the presence of your enemies.
I AM in the midst of two or three gathered in My name.
I AM God, who will answer you.
I AM the glory, who conceals a matter for a king to search out.
I AM the fountain of gardens.
I AM the resurrection of My beloved.
I AM God, whose throne is in Heaven.
I AM from above.

I AM the Lord, whose countenance beholds the upright.
I AM the just rewarder of all who seek Me.
I AM God, who teaches you to profit.
I AM the giver of abundant life.
I AM more than you can ask or think.
I AM sitting at the right hand of the Father.
I AM the Maker of many mansions therein.
I AM the Sabbath rest.
I AM the inheritance of the Levite.
I AM the fountain of life.
I AM the giver of great wisdom.
I AM the Holy Spirit, who hovers over your life to bring higher order.

 GOD OF MERCY
I AM God, who is merciful.
I AM favor, and I grant favor to whom I choose.
I AM God of the spotted and speckled.
I AM the Prince of Peace prophesied by the prophet Isaiah.
I AM God, who restores your soul.
I AM the friend of sinners.
I AM God; I tempt no one.
I AM the God of peace.
I AM He who weeps with those who weep.
I AM He who speaks from a position of mercy.
I AM long-suffering.
I AM My Spirit.
I AM gracious.
I AM the forgiver of all transgressions.
I AM the manna that came down from Heaven.
I AM the breath that gives you life.
I AM He who will not remember your sins.
I AM the beloved in the Song of Songs.
I AM God, who stretches out His hand.
I AM the liberty you seek through my Spirit.
I AM ever faithful.
I AM God in the midst of your land.
I AM the forgiver of iniquity.
I AM abundant in mercy.
I AM the altar of peace for your fear.
I AM the Lord, who makes wise the simple.
I AM God, who is daily full of new mercy.
I AM God, who comforts you.
I AM God of the poor and stranger.
I AM gentle and lowly in heart.
I AM the Lord, who exercises loving-kindness.

GOD OF EVERY CREATURE
I AM the Lord; the fear of Me is the beginning of wisdom.
I AM the God of multiplication and reproduction.
I AM Jehovah: that is My name.

I AM the God of the seraphim.
I AM the God of all flesh.
I AM the vine.
I AM the artist that all artisans draw from.
I AM Adonai Eloheynu; there is none other.
I AM the God of the cherubim.
I AM the foundation of the world.
I AM invisible, yet all creation speaks of Me.
I AM God; I want you to understand and know Me.
I AM, and you are My witnesses.
I AM glorified in you.
I AM God, who made you a sign to the unbeliever.
I AM more than all structures of steel, mortar, and clay.
I AM jealous over you.
I AM exalted head over all.
I AM God, who is joined to the foreigner.
I AM God, who speaks face-to-face.
I AM the sovereign ruler of all creation.
I AM your next breath.
I AM the light of the world.
I AM God, and all that is in Heaven and in earth is Mine.
I AM Immanuel, God dwelling among humankind.
I AM high and lifted up by all creation.
I AM the outpoured Spirit on all flesh.
I AM He who rejoices with those who rejoice.
I AM the only creator of all that exists.
I AM Savior of both the Gentiles and the Jews.
I AM He before whom every knee will bow.

GOD THE ANCIENT ONE
I AM the Lord God of Abraham, Isaac, and Jacob.
I AM the Holy Spirit, who hovered over the chaos of this earth.
I AM the light of Genesis that was before light was.
I AM the sacred Sh'ma of the ancients.
I AM the Holy One of Israel.
I AM the One whose ways are perfect.
I AM God, the fear of Me is clean, enduring forever.
I AM the Holy of Holies.
I AM the God of knowledge.
I AM the Lord, sitting on His throne.
I AM God, who formed the earth to be inhabited.
I AM understanding.
I AM God, who is joined to the eunuch.
I AM the God of all the holy prophets in Scripture.
I AM God, who divided the sea.
I AM the Lord of the dance.
I AM the Lord.
I AM the guiding star at Jesus' birth.
I AM God, who turns water into wine.
I AM He of whom all the prophets foretold.
I AM the Root of the Offspring of David.

I AM God, who leads you into all truth.
I AM God, whose rainbow is My everlasting covenant with you.
I AM the Root of Jesse.
I AM the God of Jerusalem, wherein is My name.
I AM the Creator of Israel.
I AM the God who divided the waters.
I AM the fountain of the house of David.
I AM God, who shuts up the Heavens.
I AM God, who turns water into blood.
I AM married to Israel.

 GOD THE WARRIOR
I AM the battle standard.
I AM your sharp two-edged sword.
I AM your battle cry.
I AM a warrior, and My Kingdom is spread by force.
I AM the Lord, mighty in battle.
I AM the One who annihilated Satan's plans.
I AM the Spirit of might.
I AM the master planner of all nations and kingdoms.
I AM He who leads you for My great name's sake.
I AM the conqueror of death, hell, and the grave.
I AM both warrior and poet.
I AM the Supreme God, deliverer, and possessor.
I AM the Lord of Hosts.
I AM the Kingdom, the power, and the glory.
I AM God, who cast out nations before you.
I AM commander in chief of all Heaven's armies.
I AM He who drives out the wicked before you.
I AM the defender of those who believe in Me.
I AM your strength.
I AM the Lamb sitting on the throne.
I AM your victorious banner.
I AM the fullness of greatness, power, glory, victory, and majesty.
I AM God Almighty and infinite in strength.
I AM your mighty shield.
I AM the Lion of the tribe of Judah.
I AM the sword of the Spirit.
I AM your high tower.
I AM the defender of Israel.
I AM your fortress.
I AM omnipotent.
I AM the enemy of the enemies of Israel.

INTRODUCTION

God's name is everything to a Christian. It is our heritage, our authority, our call, our vision, and our hope. It is our very life essence. We cannot exist outside the blessing of His name. His name, and the revelation of His character that it proclaims, must be seared upon our very being.

Mature Christians know that learning the names and nature of God changes us. It deepens our understanding and faith in Him. Meditating on His character changes our thought life, which in turn alters our actions. Our actions become our habits, and our habits form our destiny. By leaning on God's wisdom, power, glory, and authority, we live a life that others want to emulate.

As we influence youngsters' opinions and beliefs about God, we must remember the awesome responsibility we have been given. We must show them, in both words and actions, how God sees them. God does not see children and teenagers as insignificant; He sees them as incredibly valuable. God loves the potential in the young. He loves their energy and enthusiasm and wide-eyed wonder. He wants to know them at as young an age as possible.

Our prayer is that this curriculum will help shape young people's perspectives of God. We pray that teenagers around the world would learn more about God's character and His dreams for them. We hope to further their love for a God who loved them first.

God's name is inseparable from His glory and acts. His name prophesies of His power. We encourage you to study the names of God. Put them to work in your own life. Meditate and worship God for His power and might. Spend time with Him. And out of that fresh revelation of His Spirit, teach the young in your church of His love. Teach them first by your actions, and then with words. As we teach the next great generation, let's make Psalm 145 our prayer:

I will extol You, my God, O King;
And I will bless Your name forever and ever.
Every day I will bless You,
And I will praise Your name forever and ever.
Great is the LORD, and greatly to be praised;
And His greatness is unsearchable.

One generation shall praise Your works to another,
And shall declare Your mighty acts.
I will meditate on the glorious splendor of Your majesty,
And on Your wondrous works.
Men shall speak of the might of Your awesome acts,
And I will declare Your greatness.
They shall utter the memory of Your great goodness,
And shall sing of Your righteousness.

The LORD is gracious and full of compassion,
Slow to anger and great in mercy.
The LORD is good to all,
And His tender mercies are over all His works.
All Your works shall praise You, O LORD,
And Your saints shall bless You.
They shall speak of the glory of Your kingdom,
And talk of Your power,

To make known to the sons of men His mighty acts,
And the glorious majesty of His kingdom.
Your kingdom is an everlasting kingdom,
And Your dominion endures throughout all generations.

The LORD upholds all who fall,
And raises up all who are bowed down.
The eyes of all look expectantly to You,
And You give them their food in due season.
You open Your hand
And satisfy the desire of every living thing.

The LORD is righteous in all His ways,
Gracious in all His works.
The LORD is near to all who call upon Him,
To all who call upon Him in truth.
He will fulfill the desire of those who fear Him;
He also will hear their cry and save them.
The LORD preserves all who love Him,
But all the wicked He will destroy.
My mouth shall speak the praise of the LORD,
And all flesh shall bless His holy name
Forever and ever.

HOW TO USE THIS CURRICULUM

Teaching teenagers is always tricky. A successful teacher knows how to facilitate a conversation rather than dominate it. Unfortunately, the only way to develop your technique is to practice and prepare. Some weeks, the class will just click: there will be lots of dialogue, discussion, excitement, and positive energy. At other times, you will feel like you're pulling teeth just to get an answer. Don't give up! Keep at it! Stay the course!

To help you and your teachers become more familiar with the names of God, we strongly suggest you read John Paul Jackson's two books *I AM: 365 Names of God* and *I AM: Inheriting the Fullness of God's Name*, both available from Streams Ministries (www.streamsministries.com or 1.888.441.8080). These books will provide you with an adult understanding of the importance of the names of God, and flesh out your knowledge as you teach this material.

This curriculum can be used in any small group setting, whether it be a Sunday School class, a discipleship group, or a traditional cell group. However, this material should simply be a baseline for you. Add your own experiences and questions. You know your group far better than we ever could, so scrap the parts that you think won't work and tailor it to your young people. This material is geared to students aged eleven to sixteen.

We have discovered a few different ideas that might help you in your effort. Bribery, for example, always works. When Jennifer Bateman started a youth Sunday School at Friends Langley Vineyard Church, she knew she had to have a hook to draw the kids in. The answer: free doughnuts! For ten bucks a week, she was guaranteed a full house. Doughnuts are God's gift to curriculum writers. If this is being done at night, pizza may be a better idea. We also suggest you have candy on hand to give away when someone acts out a skit or reads a comment aloud for you.

Look for teachers. Finding people who are good with kids and are good at teaching is like finding gold. Hang on to them! Sign them to million dollar contracts if necessary. This curriculum is best taught by people who are passionate about the subject. Variety is good, too. If you can have a rotation of three or four people, that works well. Assign sessions to facilitators who understand the aspect of God you are studying: someone who has a passion for social justice could teach the weeks on sacrifice and mercy. Someone who loves to pray for miracles would be a natural fit for the session on wonders.

Be fluid. The first thing we as writers had to do was release the curriculum to other teachers. Don't be married to the words on this paper. Go where the Lord takes you. The material is just a rough guide: if a particular lesson jumped out at you, teach it. This curriculum should just be an outline of what you want to communicate.

Don't be afraid of ministry time. After studying the material, consider leading an informal prayer time based on what has been learned. Prayer for healing, boldness, vision, etc., works well with kids.

And have fun—teenagers hate it when adults are too serious!

In the attached package, you will find twelve weeks of curriculum, along with worksheets and other items that need to be photocopied. By purchasing the curriculum, you have the right to photocopy as many sheets as you need for your students. And you can pass parts of this curriculum on to other churches or pastors; just let them know that they can order the complete version from Streams Ministries (www.streamsministries.com or 1.888.441.8080). The money raised by selling this curriculum allows us to research, write, field-test, and publish more curricula.

Each session of curriculum includes an introduction page that details exactly what you will need to teach the topic.

The introduction page also includes a list of multimedia ideas for each session. The more ways material is taught, the better the chances of it being assimilated by the students. Young people respond to a variety of stimuli and techniques, so it is vital that we speak into as many of those areas as possible. Each session includes a list of songs that would fit with what is being taught. We suggest that you give each student the lyrics to those songs if you use them. There are also some sessions that have PowerPoint suggestions: simple ideas for a computer slide show. We have included some video ideas that can be accomplished by one person, with a video camera, in under an hour. Some movies and TV shows are referenced. There are also Internet suggestions, with websites and animation that can be shown during the classes. These multimedia ideas may greatly help your students' understanding of the material. Some are woven into the actual curriculum, while others can be added at your discretion.

Each session includes a Quotes and Verses handout that can be photocopied and distributed to each student. These are vital tools. Some sessions also have worksheets and skits, which are again very necessary.

Sessions begin with a brief introduction and discussion question. Discussion questions are marked with a "—>>". After the kickoff, the material looks briefly at why studying God's name is important. Later on, the curriculum moves into teaching the specific aspect of the session's particular name and attribute of God. Finally, the conclusion includes ideas for prayer or informal ministry.

A couple of sessions are slightly different form the others. I AM God of Symbols includes a plan for communion. I AM God of Mercy revolves around you planning a social justice/mercy endeavor in your community.

Dialogue is the key to the success of this material. If the class wanders off into another spiritual topic, go with them. Discuss what they want to discuss about God's nature. Don't hesitate to use their interests to further a conversation about God.

Thank you for the work you are doing. We pray that God's face will shine brightly on you and your students as you discover more about His amazing name and nature. God bless you as you praise His mighty acts to the next generation.

God of Wonders

WHAT YOU NEED

- One copy of the curriculum for the teacher
- Bibles
- One copy of the Bible Search handout for each student
- One copy of the Quotes and Verses handout for each student
- The Name Game sheet, cut, folded, and put into a hat
- A white board or big sheets of paper; pens for the Name Game
- Pens or pencils for each student

RECOMMENDED READING

Teachers would greatly benefit from reading John Paul Jackson's two books *I AM: 365 Names of God* and *I AM: Inheriting the Fullness of God's Name*, both available from Streams Ministries. John Paul Jackson reads the list of God's names on a worship/meditation CD called *I AM: 365 Names of God* which is also available from Streams.

MULTIMEDIA IDEAS

 ### POWERPOINT
Using images of creation in a PowerPoint presentation would work. We suggest www.freefoto.com/pictures/nature/index.asp, a site that allows churches and charities to use their photos freely. Another great site is www.nasa.gov, which offers stunning photos of outer space.

 ### COMPUTER ANIMATION
A California-based ministry called Highway Video produces high-quality, trendy animations for church groups. If you log on to www.highwayvideo.com and purchase their VIBE Videos, Vol. 4, you will receive five great presentations that can be used throughout this twelve-week course. For this week's class, we suggest showing "Names of God," which flashes several of God's most famous names—and their meanings—across the screen.

 ### INTERNET
Beforehand, consider pulling the meaning of students' names from a website like www.babynames.com. A good game is to pick obscure names from babynames.com and ask the students to write what they think the names mean. *The Name Book* by Dorothy Astoria is also helpful and can be ordered from Streams.

 ### MUSIC
There is plenty of music dealing with the wonders of God—we suggest handing out a list of lyrics while the songs play. Here are just a few suggestions (all of which are available at www.streamsministries.com or by calling 1.888.441.8080) that your students may enjoy:

"God of Wonders," Third Day (album: *City on a Hill*)
This song is covered by a number of different artists on various CDs

"Maker of Heaven," Flood (album: *The Well—Live in the Spirit*)

"Great God," The Wildings (album: *W2—Worship with Chris Janzen and the Wildings*)

מֹשְׁבָּה

God of Wonders

INTRODUCTION

Today, I want to talk about the importance of a name. You see, names are more than just a tag our moms and dads give us—often they reveal what type of person we are, what we believe, and even what we're good at.

>> **Does anyone here know what his or her name means?**

>> **Does that meaning hold true for the kind of person you are, or want to become?**

If you don't know what your name means, check out www.babynames.com when you get home. It's difficult to name a child. Think about people you know who have had babies. Wasn't it difficult for them to come up with a name for their child? Think of television series where characters have been pregnant—like Ross and Rachel on *Friends*, for example. They went back and forth about names for a long time before choosing Emma, which means "universal."

>> **What would you name a baby, if you could?**

>> **What would be a cool thing for a baby's name to mean?**

THE POWER OF A NAME

In biblical times, names were even more important. The Israelites really believed in what Proverbs 22:1 says [Get student to read the verse: it's on the Quotes and Verses handout, which each student should have a copy of]: "A good name is to be chosen rather than great riches. . . "

That simple proverb gives us a valuable glimpse into what Solomon and the ancient Israelites thought about the value of a name. In the Bible, a name often provided an important clue to the nature of a person or place. A person's name was linked to the type of character he or she had. People's names, quite simply, *were* their reputation.

Parents' names for their children often expressed their dreams for those babies. Children were named with the hope that they would become what their name meant. For example, if a boy's mother and father named him David, which means "beloved," they hoped the baby would grow to be a person who was loved by God and people. In naming a child, many Israelites believed a name had the ability to shape the child's destiny.

Jesus carried on this tradition in the New Testament, when he renamed His friend Simon in Matthew 16:17–18 [Get student to read the verse: it's on the Quotes and Verses handout, which each student should have a copy of]: "Jesus answered and said to him, 'Blessed are you, Simon Bar–Jonah, for flesh and blood has not revealed this to you, but My Father who is in heaven. And I also say to you that you are Peter, and on this rock I will build My church, and the gates of Hades shall not prevail against it.' "

Jesus took the name *Peter*, from *petros*, the Greek word for "rock," and gave it to His friend as a prophetic word of Simon's future in the Kingdom of God. He would be a rock that the whole Church could be built on—strong and steady.

> ——>> **What name would you rather have, Peter (meaning "rock") or Simon (meaning "it is heard")?**

This wasn't the first time God had changed the name of one of His friends. In Genesis 17:5, God spoke to Abram [Get student to read the verse: it's on the Quotes and Verses handout, which each student should have a copy of]: "No longer shall your name be called Abram, but your name shall be Abraham; for I have made you a father of many nations."

> ——>> **What name would you rather have, Abraham ("father of many nations") or Abram (simply "father")?**

A few years later, in Genesis 32:28, God renamed Abraham's grandson Jacob [Get student to read the verse: it's on the Quotes and Verses handout, which each student should have a copy of]: "Your name shall no longer be called Jacob, but Israel; for you have struggled with God and with men, and have prevailed." Israel means "Prince of God."

There are some downright strange names in the Bible too. In fact, their meanings are just bizarre. They are, though, deadly accurate about what kind of person or place they depict.

NAME GAME

I have a game that will help show you this. We're going to play Pictionary, and I need the guys and girls to split up into teams, guys over here, and girls over there. Each team will be given two Bible name meanings, and they must draw out the name meanings. You have sixty seconds.

Boys will go first. I need a volunteer to pick the first name.

[Have the boys pick out a name from the hat and draw it; then the girls, and so on. If the two teams are tied after four names, have volunteers from both teams to pick the fifth name. First team to draw it out, wins. Have some candy on hand as a prize.]

Let's look at the names you've drawn and see what they mean:

"Fool" was the meaning of the name of a man named Nabal (1 Samuel 25:25).

"Mother of All" was the meaning of the name of Eve (Genesis 3:20).

"A Group Will Return" was the meaning of the name of Isaiah's son Shear-Jashub (Isaiah 7:3).

"The Fruit of Victory" was the meaning of the name of Isaiah's son Maher-Shalal-Hash-Baz (Isaiah 8:1).

"Babble" was the meaning of the name of the tower of Babel, where God created new languages (Genesis 11:9).

GOD OF WONDERS

If human names were so important to God that He would actually rename people, how much more important must His own name be? Just look at the depth of character contained in the hundreds of names God has given Himself.

One of the themes of God's names is that He is the God of Wonders. God's wonders never change. His power and powerful acts are the same yesterday, today, and tomorrow. He is in control of the universe—showing His compassionate and mighty acts in thousands of ways.

> **——>> What are some of the wonders God does or has made?**

The Bible is jam-packed with examples of the wondrous things God does. Let's look at just a few.

He is the God who shows us wonders, says Acts 2:19 *[Get student to read the verse: it's on the Quotes and Verses handout, which each student should have a copy of]*: "I will show wonders in heaven above and signs in the earth beneath: blood and fire and vapor of smoke."
That's an amazing picture of the power of God. He gives us wonders in the sky—like the star over Bethlehem when Jesus was born, and the manna that fell from Heaven when the Israelites were wandering in the desert.

——>> **Has anyone here thought about God when looking up into a beautiful sky?**

——>> **What does it feel like when you look at a beautiful sunset, or when you see rays of sunlight streaming through gray clouds?**

He is also the God of all flesh, meaning every man, woman, and child. Let's read Jeremiah 32:27 *[Get student to read the verse: it's on the Quotes and Verses handout, which each student should have a copy of]*: "Behold, I am the LORD, the God of all flesh. Is there anything too hard for Me?"

——>> **Is there anything too hard for God?**

——>> **Is there something you've never asked Him for help on, because you didn't think He would or could?**

Here's a verse describing the kind of wondrous power that Jesus would walk in. It's Isaiah 11:2 *[Get student to read the verse: it's on the Quotes and Verses handout, which each student should have a copy of]*: "The Spirit of the LORD shall rest upon Him, the Spirit of wisdom and understanding, the Spirit of counsel and might, the Spirit of knowledge and of the fear of the LORD."

This is an interesting verse, because it explains so much to us about how Jesus lived and acted. He was wise and understanding; full of good advice and strength; smart and in love with God the Father. As Christians, we are called to be "little Christs," emulating Jesus in every possible way.

——>> **If you could be just one of these things, which would you choose: wise, understanding, good with advice, strong, or smart?**

——>> **How could that gift help you, your family, your friends, and your youth group?**

WORKSHEET

(Photocopy the attached Bible Search, one for each student. The questions can also be discussed in the full group setting; hopefully, some good conversation will be sparked.)

I AM GOD OF WONDERS BIBLE SEARCH

In Exodus 18:11, we read: "Now I know that the LORD is greater than all the gods; for in the very thing in which they have behaved proudly, He was above them." What we're being taught here is that the smallest of God's wonders surpass even the greatest human accomplishments and efforts—He's that far above us in ability and power.

Below is a list of five wonders of God we can find in the Bible. *[In groups of three or four, write down how you would explain that piece of God's greatness to a friend of yours who had never heard of Him. Then discuss the question underneath each line.]*

1. "The preparations of the heart belong to man, but the answer of the tongue is from the LORD." (Proverbs 16:1)

_____

_____

Discussion question: Have you ever given an answer that you knew **was** from God? Have you ever given an answer that you knew **wasn't** from God?

2. "I am the LORD who heals you." (Exodus 15:26)

_____

_____

Discussion question: Have you ever seen God heal someone? Has He ever healed you?

3. "Thus says the LORD, your Redeemer, and He who formed you from the womb . . . " (Isaiah 44:24)

_____

_____

Discussion question: What does it mean to be "formed from" the womb? What do you think God does in there?

4. "Sing to God, sing praises to His name; extol Him who rides on the clouds." (Psalm 68:4a)

_____

_____

Discussion question: What does it mean to "ride on the clouds"? What would that be like?

5. "Then He said, 'If there is a prophet among you, I, the LORD, make Myself known to him in a vision; I speak to him in a dream.' " (Numbers 12:6)

_____

_____

Discussion question: Has God ever spoken to you in a dream or a vision? What was it like?

MINISTRY TIME

[There are a few ways to wrap this session up, depending on the nature of your class. One is simply to pray and conclude. You could also ask for prayer requests, and pray for those items. A more in-depth ministry time might include you praying for God's wonders to be revealed to the students. I would reread Numbers 12:6, "Then He said, 'If there is a prophet among you, I, the Lord, make Myself known to him in a vision; I speak to him in a dream.'" Then pray that God would reveal His wondrous power to the kids through dreams and visions that week. Next week, ask the students if any of them had a dream or encounter with God's power this week. You'll be surprised how many did.]

I AM GOD OF WONDERS

Cut out all the strips and put in a hat for the Name Game. Don't let the students see the list until it's time for him or her to draw.

Fool

Mother of All

A Group Will Return

The Fruit of Victory

Babble

I AM GOD OF WONDERS BIBLE SEARCH

In **Exodus 18:11**, we read: **"Now I know that the LORD is greater than all the gods; for in the very thing in which they behaved proudly, He was above them."** What we're being taught here is that the smallest of God's wonders surpass even the greatest human accomplishments and efforts—He's that far above us in ability and power.

Below is a list of five of the wonders of God we can find in the Bible. **In groups of three or four, write down how you would explain that piece of God's greatness to a friend of yours who had never heard of Him. Then discuss the question underneath each line.**

1. "The preparations of the heart belong to man, but the answer of the tongue is from the LORD." (Proverbs 16:1)

_____

_____

*Discussion question: Have you ever given an answer that you knew **was** from God? Have you ever given an answer that you knew **wasn't** from God?*

2. "I am the LORD who heals you." (Exodus 15:26)

_____

_____

Discussion question: Have you ever seen God heal someone? Has He ever healed you?

3. "Thus says the LORD, your Redeemer, and He who formed you from the womb . . . " (Isaiah 44:24)

_____

_____

Discussion question: What does it mean to be "formed from" the womb? What do you think God does in there?

4. "Sing to God, sing praises to His name; extol Him who rides on the clouds." (Psalm 68:4)

_____

_____

Discussion question: What does it mean to "ride on the clouds"? What would that be like?

5. "Then He said, 'If there is a prophet among you, I, the LORD, make Myself known to him in a vision; I speak to him in a dream.' "(Numbers 12:6)

_____

_____

Discussion question: Has God ever spoken to you in a dream or a vision? What was it like?

I AM GOD OF WONDERS

Proverbs 22:1
"A good name is to be chosen rather than great riches . . . "

Matthew 16:17–18
"Jesus answered and said to him, 'Blessed are you, Simon Bar-Jonah, for flesh and blood has not revealed this to you, but My Father who is in heaven. And I also say to you that you are Peter, and on this rock I will build My church, and the gates of Hades shall not prevail against it.'"

Genesis 17:5
"No longer shall your name be called Abram, but your name shall be Abraham; for I have made you a father of many nations."

Genesis 32:28
"Your name shall no longer be called Jacob, but Israel; for you have struggled with God and with men, and have prevailed."

Acts 2:19
"I will show wonders in heaven above and signs in the earth beneath: blood and fire and vapor of smoke."

Jeremiah 32:27
"Behold, I am the LORD, the God of all flesh. Is there anything too hard for Me?"

Isaiah 11:2
"The Spirit of the LORD shall rest upon Him, the Spirit of wisdom and understanding, the Spirit of counsel and might, the Spirit of knowledge and of the fear of the LORD."

God of Justice

WHAT YOU NEED

- One copy of the curriculum for the teacher
- Bibles
- One copy of the Quotes and Verses handout for each student
- Four copies of the Skits handout
- Pens or pencils for each student

RECOMMENDED READING

Teachers would greatly benefit from reading John Paul Jackson's two books *I AM: 365 Names of God* and *I AM: Inheriting the Fullness of God's Name*, both available from Streams Ministries (www.streamsministries.com or 1.888.441.8080). *I AM: 365 Names of God* is also available on a worship/meditation CD from Streams.

MULTIMEDIA IDEAS

 ### VIDEO
Videotape a few court shows during the week (*Judge Judy, Judge Joe Brown, People's Court*). Find the funniest segment on any of the shows, and bring it in for the students to watch. The more outlandish, the better.

 ### INTERNET
A great website to discover social justice issues on is www.cred.tv, a ministry based in the United Kingdom. Consider pulling information from this site for the kids to consider.

Another popular website is www.data.org, which outlines Bono's and U2's attempts to help developing African nations. This organization has received much press and may already be known to some of your students.

 ### SONGS
"Did You Feel the Mountains Tremble?" by Delirious (available on *Cutting Edge*) is a song that many youth groups have adopted as a pro-God's justice anthem.

צֶדֶק

God of Justice

INTRODUCTION

Last time, we looked at how God is the God of Wonders, performing miracles today, just as He did in the Bible. Today, we're going to examine how the justice of God works, and how we can prompt Him to help us.

—>> **Do you want God to act on your behalf in situations and troubles that face you? Why?**

God is the God of Justice. He loves righteousness, and He has set up a system of how the universe works. We are all subject to it, but it isn't confining or frightening as we might think—God's pure justice actually keeps us safe and secure in Him.

First, however, let's take a few minutes to learn more about why it is so important to take the time to explore the names of God.

THE IMPORTANCE OF GOD'S NAMES

For millennia, many Israelites had so much respect for God's name that they wouldn't even use it—they thought it was too precious for humans to say! When God introduced Himself to Abraham, He used the name *Yahweh*, but it was thought the name was too holy to pronounce, or to record.

—>> **Do you think having this much respect for God's name was a good thing, or a bad thing? Why?**

—>> **What sort of challenges would we face today if we never said or wrote God's name?**

The names of God tell us a lot about His character and His love for us. These names must be respected, because they are examples of God's glory and reputation. In sharing His name with us, God presents Himself as a real, live Person in order to build a friendship with us. Not only is God revealing Himself in a personal way, He is also revealing His character and reputation to you and me.

—>> **Can you be friends with someone if you don't know his or her name or nature?**

—>> **What do your friends' reputations tell you about them?**

By telling us His name, God was giving us the chance to receive the protection, blessing, and covering that His name provides. Why is this important? For two reasons: it is an invitation for friendship and it allows us to ask for His help.

First, God's desire to be known in a personal way reveals an important aspect of His character. He wants to enter into a friendship with His creation. God has invited any and all to call out His name and experience the blessings it will bring.

It is amazing that the Creator of the universe would want to become part of the very world He made. He took on a name so that He could be known and loved by His creation.

—>> **What is it about His creation that God loves so much?**

Nowhere is God's desire for friendship more obvious than in His decision to send His Son, Jesus, to earth [*Get the kids to read: John 3:16 on the Quotes and Verses handout*]: "For God so loved the world that He gave His only begotten Son, that whoever believes in Him should not perish but have everlasting life." God's name was carried boldly and completely by Jesus, as an example to us of how we can have relationship with the Father.

—>> **What did Jesus' life show us about God the Father?**

Not only does God offer us the blessing of knowing Him personally, but He also offers us the influence, favor, and protection that His name carries. God is the King of all the earth. As such,

36

He can offer us the eternal protection and blessing of His name, both in this life and in Heaven. All we need to do is believe in His name. In the New Testament, we are told that if we call upon the name of the Lord, we will experience the saving power of God, both physically and spiritually *[Have a student read Acts 2:21 on the Quotes and Verses handout]*: " . . . that whoever calls on the name of the LORD shall be saved."

God loves to come close to His children and give them the benefits of His name *[Have a student read Exodus 20:24 on the Quotes and Verses handout]*: "In every place where I record My name I will come to you, and I will bless you."

> **——>> Have you ever taken God up on this promise—that where you call on His name, He'll come and bless you? Tell us about it.**

GOD OF JUSTICE

God loves justice, because it is who He is. He is completely just and righteous—even a quick look through the Bible can show us this aspect of who He is. *[Have a student read Psalm 98:9 on the Quotes and Verses handout]*: "For He is coming to judge the earth. With righteousness He shall judge the world, and the peoples with equity." *[Have another student read 2 Chronicles 12:6 on the Quotes and Verses handout]*: "So the leaders of Israel and the king humbled themselves; and they said, 'The LORD is righteous.'"

The problem we run into is that we have a bad view of what justice is.

> **——>> What comes to your mind when I say the word *Judge*?**

> **——>> What comes to your mind when we talk about *Justice*?**

It's easy for us to equate God's justice with what we see on courtroom TV shows like *Judge Judy* or the *People's Court,* or what we read in the newspaper about evil people going free. But God's justice system doesn't work that way. It is as far above our system as Heaven is above the earth. Here, I have a skit that helps illustrate this—may I have four volunteers, please?

SKITS
Select actors to play the four roles, and hand them the sheets they need.

CHARACTERS
The Judge
The Prosecutor
The Defense Attorney
The Defendant
The Narrator (should be the group facilitator)

SETTING

Judge should sit on a chair at the front of the room facing the group while the two attorneys—the Prosecutor to the Judge's left and the Defense Attorney to the Judge's right—sit facing him or her with their backs to the room. The Defendant should sit next to the Defense Attorney. The Narrator may be anywhere.

SKIT

Narrator (*loudly, as an introduction to the group*): One of the big problems in the world today is that people have a wrong view of God and what His nature as a righteous judge means for us. We're afraid of Him, because we think He's out to get us. Watch the following skits and ask yourself the question, "Is this how I think of God?"

Judge: I call this session of court to order. Prosecutor, what do you have to say about this defendant?

Prosecutor: Your Honor, this defendant must be punished severely! We the people demand justice!

Judge: Really? What has he/she done?

Prosecutor: In Grade six, he/she read a note that was being passed from Melanie Thomson to Kelly Handsfield! That's invasion of privacy!

Judge (*very angry*): He/she did what?!? That's a year in jail!

Prosecutor: Then, in Grade seven, he/she stole ten dollars from his/her mom's purse!

Judge (*still upset*): No! No! No! He/she did? I can't believe it! Another two years behind bars!

Prosecutor: In Grade two, he/she didn't finish his/her sandwich—he/she fed the rest to his/her dog!

Defense Attorney: Objection, Your Honor!

Defendant: It was bologna! I hate bologna!

Judge: Be quiet! That's another three years in prison! I can't believe you wasted food! What else have you got, Prosecutor?

Prosecutor: He/she gets bored in church every Sunday! He/she missed youth group to see a movie!

Judge: This makes me sick! Lock him/her up and throw away the key!

Defendant: Isn't this a little harsh? It's not like I murdered someone . . .

Defense Attorney: Shhh, you'll make the judge angrier!

Prosecutor: Be quiet! Or I'll play the videotape of your first so-called kiss! It'll be embarrassing, how you tripped and fell! All of us will laugh and ridicule you for years!

Defendant: No, please, no more! Just lock me up—it's all true, I'm evil. Evil!

Prosecutor: Your Honor, we rest our case.

Defense Attorney: Sir, there is nothing I can say to excuse my client's choices in life. The defense rests.

Judge: I hereby sentence you to life in prison without parole. Get out of my sight, you monster!

Narrator (*loudly to the group*): Sadly, that really is how many of us perceive God's judgment in our lives. When things are bad, we think it's Him spanking us. But here is a more accurate representation of how God judges us.

Judge: I call this session of court to order. Prosecutor, what are the charges against this defendant?

Prosecutor: Your Honor, this defendant must be punished severely! We demand justice!

Judge: Really? What has he/she done?

Prosecutor: In Grade six, he/she stole his/her best friend's lint brush. That's breaking and entering, Your Honor!

Judge (*looking at Defendant*): Wait a minute. Don't I know you? What's your name, child?

Defendant: My name is _____.

Judge: I do know you! I love you! How have you been?

Defendant: Good, Your Honor.

Prosecutor: Er, Your Honor, may we get back to the point? This person is a criminal and needs to be locked up.

Judge: Are you kidding me. I love _____. He/she has the best sense of humor. He/she is kind, fun, intelligent and full of life. Why would I ever punish him/her?

Defense Attorney: Well said, Your Honor.

Prosecutor (*very frustrated*): But Your Honor, that's not right! He/she does bad things! He/she stole a lint brush and doesn't make his/her bed every morning! He/she is evil!

Judge: I'm sick and tired of your accusations, Mr. Prosecutor. Maybe I should lock you up! As for _____, he/she is free to go, with the love and respect of this court. If you need anything, just call—I want to help you.

Narrator (*loudly to the group*): Let's give these actors a hand.

GOD OF JUSTICE, PART TWO

God has spiritual laws that govern everything in the universe. He says don't murder, so we must not murder. He says don't lie, so we must not lie. His laws are not difficult or tough but fair and based on Jesus' two rules: love God, and love one another. God's laws allow Him to love us completely and fully. If we follow those spiritual laws, we'll receive blessings; but if we ignore them, we'll be cursed. Fulfilling God's commands brings us hope and freedom.

Some people think Christianity is just one stupid rule after another, but nothing could be further from the truth. In hockey, there are rules, but those rules give structure and purpose to the game. Score more goals than the other team and you win. Hit someone with a high stick and you are penalized. In basketball, you can't walk with the ball—it's traveling. You can't punch a guy in the back of the head as he goes for a lay-up. In football, it is illegal to pull a guy down by his face mask. These rules govern the games and make the world of sports possible.

So it is with God's justice system. His spiritual laws bring us hope and freedom. [*Have a student read Psalm 19:8 on the Quotes and Verses handout*]: "The statutes of the Lord are right, rejoicing the heart; the commandment of the LORD is pure, enlightening the eyes." God's laws brighten our eyes—they make us happy and safe in His protection. They make our hearts happy.

> —>> **Can anyone give me an example of one of God's laws that makes us happy?**

God does not have good days and cranky days. He doesn't sit in Heaven like Judge Judy, get mad one day, and start calling down judgment. Just the opposite—He loves His justice system and He loves the way it works. Look at Genesis 18:25 [*have a student read it aloud; it's on the Quotes and Verses handout*]: "Far be it from You to do such a thing as this, to slay the right-eous with the wicked, so that the righteous should be as the wicked; far be it from You! Shall not the Judge of all the earth do right?"

> —>> **What does the God of Justice want from you?**

> —>> **What are some of the spiritual laws He has given us to follow?**

> —>> **Are you fulfilling the spiritual laws He has given?** *Do we love our neighbor, for example?*

God's justice system actually helps us greatly. When something bad happens to us, we know that God is fair—for every evil, He will deliver good, and more. If you're mistreated, you can trust that God will reverse that sin, and turn it into a positive in your life. He'll even give you a reward for your pain and suffering. Where many of us fall down is that we aren't patient enough to let God work. Instead, we jump in and try to fight back ourselves—leaving God no room to work. By trying to punish evildoers ourselves, we actually miss out on His blessing. We can't pick and choose the spiritual laws we want to obey. God wants us to follow them all, because He wants to give us all the blessings He can.

MINISTRY TIME AND CONCLUSION

[Be sensitive to your group. Some prayer requests and prayer may be sufficient, but if they are ready to dig deeper, by all means go with them.]

★ ★ ★

I AM GOD OF JUSTICE

John 3:16
"For God so loved the world that He gave His only begotten Son, that whoever believes in Him should not perish but have everlasting life."

Acts 2:21
" . . . That whoever calls on the name of the LORD shall be saved."

Exodus 20:24
"In every place where I record My name I will come to you, and I will bless you."

Psalm 98:9
"For He is coming to judge the earth. With righteousness He shall judge the world, and the peoples with equity."

2 Chronicles 12:6
"So the leaders of Israel and the king humbled themselves; and they said, 'The LORD is righteous.'"

Psalm 19:8
"The statutes of the LORD are right, rejoicing the heart; the commandment of the Lord is pure, enlightening the eyes."

Genesis 18:25
"Far be it from You to do such a thing as this, to slay the righteous with the wicked, so that the righteous should be as the wicked; far be it from You! Shall not the Judge of all the earth do right?"

SESSION 2 | SKIT #1

I AM GOD OF JUSTICE

CHARACTERS
The Judge
The Prosecutor
The Defense Attorney
The Defendant
The Narrator (should be the group facilitator)

SETTING
Judge should sit on a chair at the front of the room facing the group while the two attorneys—the Prosecutor to the Judge's left and the Defense Attorney to the Judge's right—sit facing him or her, with their backs to the room. The Defendant should sit next to the Defense Attorney. The Narrator may be anywhere.

SKIT

Narrator *(loudly, as an introduction to the group)*: One of the big problems in the world today is that people have a wrong view of God and what His nature as a righteous judge means for us. We're afraid of Him, because we think He's out to get us. Watch the following skits and ask yourself the question, "Is this how I think of God?"

Judge: I call this session of court to order. Prosecutor, what do you have to say about this defendant?

Prosecutor: Your Honor, this defendant must be punished severely! We the people demand justice!

Judge: Really? What has he/she done?

Prosecutor: In Grade six, he/she read a note that was being passed from Melanie Thomson to Kelly Handsfield! That's invasion of privacy!

Judge *(very angry)*: He/she did what?!? That's a year in jail!

Prosecutor: Then, in Grade seven, he/she stole ten dollars from his/her mom's purse!

Judge *(still upset)*: No! No! No! He/she did? I can't believe it! Another two years behind bars!

Prosecutor: In Grade two, he/she didn't finish his/her sandwich—he/she fed the rest to his/her dog!

Defense Attorney: Objection, Your Honor!

Defendant: It was bologna! I hate bologna!

Judge: Be quiet! That's another three years in prison! I can't believe you wasted food! What else have you got, Prosecutor?

Prosecutor: He/she gets bored in church every Sunday! He/she missed youth group to see a movie!

Judge: This makes me sick! Lock him/her up and throw away the key!

Defendant: Isn't this a little harsh? It's not like I murdered someone . . .

Defense Attorney: Shhh, you'll make the judge angrier!

Prosecutor: Be quiet! Or I'll play the videotape of your first so-called kiss! It'll be embarrassing, how you tripped and fell! All of us will laugh and ridicule you for years!

Defendant: No, please, no more! Just lock me up—it's all true, I'm evil. Evil!

Prosecutor: Your Honor, we rest our case.

Defense Attorney: Sir, there is nothing I can say to excuse my client's choices in life. The defense rests.

Judge: I hereby sentence you to life in prison without parole. Get out of my sight, you monster!

Narrator (*loudly to the group*): Sadly, that really is how many of us perceive God's judgment in our lives. When things are bad, we think it's Him spanking us. But here is a more accurate representation of how God judges us.

Judge: I call this session of court to order. Prosecutor, what are the charges against this defendant?

Prosecutor: Your Honor, this defendant must be punished severely! We demand justice!

Judge: Really? What has he/she done?

Prosecutor: In Grade six, he/she stole his/her best friend's lint brush. That's breaking and entering, Your Honor!

Judge (*looking at Defendant*): Wait a minute. Don't I know you? What's your name, child?

Defendant: My name is _____.

Judge: I do know you! I love you! How have you been?

Defendant: Good, Your Honor.

Prosecutor: Er, Your Honor, may we get back to the point? This person is a criminal and needs to be locked up.

Judge: Are you kidding me. I love _____. He/she has the best sense of humor. He/she is kind, fun, intelligent and full of life. Why would I ever punish him/her?

Defense Attorney: Well said, Your Honor.

Prosecutor (*very frustrated*): But Your Honor, that's not right! He/she does bad things! He/she stole a lint brush and doesn't make his/her bed every morning! He/she is evil!

Judge: I'm sick and tired of your accusations, Mr. Prosecutor. Maybe I should lock you up! As for _____, he/she is free to go, with the love and respect of this court. If you need anything, just call—I want to help you.

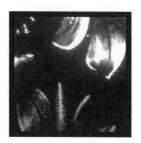

God of Symbols

WHAT YOU NEED

- Communion elements—enough bread and grape juice for everyone in the class
- One copy of the curriculum for the teacher
- Bibles
- One copy of the Quotes and Verses handout for each student
- One copy of the Game handout for the teacher
- Timer (a kid's watch will suffice)
- Prizes for the game are always a good idea
- Pens or pencils for each student

RECOMMENDED READING

Teachers would greatly benefit from reading John Paul Jackson's two books *I AM: 365 Names of God* and *I AM: Inheriting the Fullness of God's Name*, both available from Streams Ministries (www.streamsministries.com or 1.888.441.8080). *I AM: 365 Names of God* is also available on a worship/meditation CD from Streams.

MULTIMEDIA IDEAS

VISUALS

On *Vibe Video, Vol. 4*, available from www.highwayvideo.com, there is a very cool presentation called "Symbols of Reverence." This could loop throughout your time together.

A controversial yet conversation-provoking look at materialism in North America can be found at https://secure.adbusters.org/orders/flag. This artwork puts corporate logos and symbols into an American flag. It would undoubtedly lead to an interesting discussion with students about symbolism and materialism.

A free, downloadable Windows Media file showing a glass of wine, a piece of bread, and a candle is available at http://emergingminister.com/video/communion.mpg. This would be a nice graphic to display during communion.

VIDEOS

Take ten minutes and walk through your town with a video camera. Tape every symbol you can find: traffic lights, logos, flags, stop signs. Show the video to the students, and see how many symbols they can recognize.

Videotape a bunch of TV commercials throughout the week. Ask kids to shout out—as soon as they know it—what each ad is advertising. You'll be stunned at how many they can name in fewer than five seconds.

MUSIC

Two great songs can be found on CDs available from Streams Ministries (www.streamsministries.com or call 1.888.441.8080):

"Big Ocean" from The Wildings' *Wild-Eyed Wonder* album, is a song packed with symbolism. It can be played and allowed to lead into the next song on the CD, "Fall on Me," a beautiful worship piece.

"This Road," a song by Jars of Clay on the *City on a Hill* album, is also chock-full of symbolism.

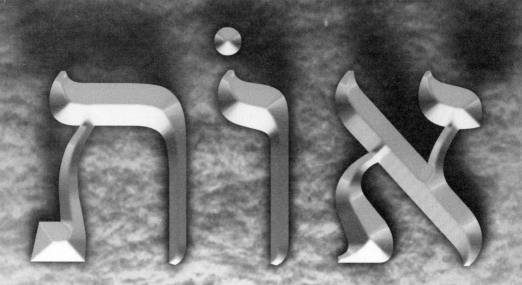

God of Symbols

INTRODUCTION

God is a God of Symbols—He loves to hide His deepest truth in the simplest of metaphors. Symbols are everywhere—but today, we call them logos.

—>> **What does a Swoosh symbolize? (Nike)**

—>> **What does a red light symbolize? (Stop)**

—>> **What TV station is symbolized by a peacock? (NBC)**

—>> **What is your favorite sports team symbol?**

—>> **What does Pepsi's symbol look like?**

—>> **Why do we have so many symbols?**

Symbols give us a shortcut to understanding the things they stand for. God is no different; He wanted humans to know who He was, so He placed dozens of symbols in the Bible to offer little glimpses of truth about His name and nature.

THE IMPORTANCE OF GOD'S NAMES

Before we talk more about the symbolism God uses to help us understand Him, let's take a quick look at what it means to carry God's name on our lives. By calling ourselves Christians, we are saying that we are "like Christ;" that He is our defining characteristic. We are also saying that He has set us apart for something special.

> ——>> **What has God set us apart to be? What has He set us apart to do?**

God's names, His acts, and His glory are all inseparable. We cannot take God's names away from His acts or His glory. His names describe who He is throughout time, and they describe what He has done and will do. For example, God, who was once Jehovah Rapha (which means the Lord heals), is not now ex-Jehovah Rapha. He is not the artist formerly known as Jehovah Rapha. He is still Jehovah Rapha, the Lord who heals. He was, He is, and He will be continually Jehovah Rapha.

I have a great picture of what this means in life. Close your eyes and picture this scene. There is a beautiful valley, full of flowers and water and green grass, surrounded by tall, icy mountains. In the valley, there is an army marching—there are thousands of troops, marching like a penetrating, focused laser beam. In front of them is a huge flame, so large that it looks like a burning cloud. They are a powerful army, led by the fire of God's presence.

Now look into the mountains and see the enemy kings, watching this. Their knees knock together as they see the supernatural cloud of flame rising into the Heavens. Knowing they face an incredibly powerful and unified army, the kings try to hide their fear as they issue commands to their troops. In their hearts, they know this battle is a lost cause, for they are about to war against God Himself.

Open your eyes—this is a true story.

> ——>> **Who can tell me where we find this story in the Bible?**

[Have a student read Exodus 13:21–22; it's on the Quotes and Verses handout]: "And the Lord went before them by day in a pillar of cloud to lead the way, and by night in a pillar of fire to give them light, so as to go by day and night. He did not take away the pillar of cloud by day or the pillar of fire by night from before the people."

God's glory was marching before the army. In the Bible, we are told that Moses and the Israelites' journey through the desert was led by a cloud by day and a fire by night. We are told that this was the glory of God showing itself to, and guiding, them. With God before them, who could stop them?

Now close your eyes again, while I describe another scene. It's the same valley and the same army, but this time the soldiers are scattered like pepper on the floor. Some are walking up into the mountainsides. Some are walking too far ahead. Some are walking off to the side. And some are lingering behind. This group is not walking in unison.

Now scan the valley for the cloud and the pillar of fire that was supposed to lead them—it's nowhere near as powerful as it once was; in fact, it's just a thin, insubstantial wisp that is barely recognizable. The people's disbelief, dysfunction, and disunity have allowed God's leadership in their lives almost to disappear.

Now look along the mountainsides and see the same enemies looking down over the group of people. These enemies aren't afraid. In fact, they are like vultures that have just spied an easy prey. They are licking their chops with excitement over their impending victory.

Okay, open your eyes again.

—>> **Which army would you prefer to be a part of?**

—>> **What is it about God that makes His enemies so frightened?**

The first group was God's people, Israel, when they came out of Egypt. The kings of the lands they invaded saw them and were terrified. God's glory was with them.

Unfortunately, the second group of people is what happens when we reduce God's glory to a thin wisp of smoke. No one fears Him—or His people—anymore. By reducing the way we expect—and allow—God to operate, we have taken away some of His glory. By putting God into a convenient, understandable box, we have separated His name, His acts, and His glory, weakening all three.

We strip God of His glory by saying that His attributes no longer exist today. For example, some say that God no longer predicts the future. So they take this part of His name and place it to the side. Others say that God no longer delivers. Or that God no longer heals or even cares. Every Christian, at some point in his or her life, has deleted or distorted pieces of God's incredible glory, casting it aside like an old, worn-out pair of shoes.

—>> **How do we reduce God's glory?**

—>> **In worship, do we really believe some of the songs we are singing?**

—>> **What aspect of God's nature would you most like to discover over the next few months?**

GOD OF SYMBOLS
We can learn a lot about God's nature when we study the many symbols He put into the Bible. The Bible is full of these symbols. Let's look at a few . . . by acting them out.

GAME
[Split the group into two teams; boys versus girls is always an easy way.]
This game is simple. I'll give a word to one member of your team; he or she will act it out—without saying a word or humming or making any sound or pointing at anything in the room—and your team has forty-five seconds to guess it. It's charades! If one side doesn't get it at the end of forty-five seconds, the other team may steal by answering correctly—they only get one

guess at it, though. Remember, these are all symbols used in the Bible to describe God.

[The words are on the Game sheet; be careful to show each actor only one:
Light
Star
Judge
Fire
Rock
Door
Fountain
Water
The tiebreaker word is Oil; have both teams compete on this one simultaneously.]

GAME OUTFLOW
Let's look at where these terms came from, shall we? We'll start with *Light. [Have student read 1 John 1:5; all these verses are on their Quotes and Verses handout]: "This is the message which we have heard from Him and declare to you, that God is light and in Him is no darkness at all."*

>> **What can we figure out about light that tells us something about God?**

Now let's look at *Star. [Have a student read Revelation 22:16: It's on the Quotes and Verses handout]: "I, Jesus, have sent My angel to testify to you these things in the churches. I am the Root and the Offspring of David, the Bright and Morning Star."*

>> **What does this symbol—and the others mentioned—tell us about Jesus?**

Last time, we studied how God is a God of Justice. Today, we had the word *Judge. [Have a student read Psalm 75:6–7: It's on the Quotes and Verses handout]: "For exaltation comes neither from the east nor from the west nor from the south. But God is the Judge: He puts down one, and exalts another."*

>> **What does it mean to put down one, and exalt another?**

Let's look at *Water. [Have a student read John 4:14: It's on the Quotes and Verses handout]: "But whoever drinks of the water that I shall give him will never thirst. But the water that I shall give him will become in him a fountain of water springing up into everlasting life."*

>> **What is the water Jesus gives us?**

Okay, *Rock. [Have a student read 1 Corinthians 10:4 on the Quotes and Verses handout]: "For they drank of that spiritual Rock that followed them, and that Rock was Christ."*

>> **What qualities of a rock does God share?**

Now, *Door. [Have a student read John 10:9 on the Quotes and Verses handout.]: "I am the door. If anyone enters by Me, he will be saved, and will go in and out and find pasture."*

—>> **What does loving Jesus open our lives to?**

Three more. Let's look at *Fountain*. [*Have a student read Psalm 68:26 on the Quotes and Verses handout*]: "Bless God in the congregations, the Lord, from the fountain of Israel."

—>> **How can our worship be like a fountain before God?**

Fire. [*Have a student read Deuteronomy 4:24 on the Quotes and Verses handout*]: "For the Lord your God is a consuming fire, a jealous God."

—>> **What does this symbol mean?**

The last one, it was the tiebreaker: *Oil*. [*Have a student read Leviticus 21:12 on the Quotes and Verses handout*]: "For the consecration of the anointing oil of his God is upon him: I am the Lord."

—>> **What does consecration mean?**

GOD OF SYMBOLS, PART TWO

As we have read, the Bible is full of symbols used to describe God. These give us a glimpse of who He is, and what He loves to do.

—>> **Why do you think He spent so much time trying to describe Himself?**

—>> **Why did He choose symbols to do that?**

Perhaps the greatest symbol God gave us was the bread and wine of communion. In the hours before Jesus was arrested and crucified, He and His disciples gathered for a Last Supper, a Passover seder. They sat and ate and laughed and shared their hopes, dreams, and ideas. In the midst of it all, Jesus became serious.

As they ate, Jesus took bread, blessed it, broke it, and handed it to His friends. "This is My body," He said, "Broken for you." They didn't know it then, but a few days later, Jesus' body really would be broken for them—His death on the cross was the turning point of history, the moment that opened the door for men and women to experience eternal life. He called Himself the bread of life, a picture of how we need to feed on Jesus to survive, to fulfill our most basic spiritual needs.

Later at the Last Supper, He took the wine, gave thanks to God for it, and poured it into the cups of His disciples. "For this is My blood of the new covenant, which is shed for many for the remission of sins," He said. By His death, Jesus' sacrifice would redeem humankind, bringing us into a new and deeper relationship with God.

Bread and wine, two of the simplest and most common items in the world, were made more than that: they are symbols of God's never-ending love for us. That's the power of God's symbolism—it makes real the mystical.

COMMUNION AND CONCLUSION

[Take communion together—using whatever form your church usually takes; this is part of handing down millennia of tradition. Be serious but not morose; remember this is a feast, not a funeral.]

[If you are unsure of how to serve communion, simply pray, read the following passage aloud (1 Corinthians 11:23–26, NIV), and take the bread and juice.]

["The Lord Jesus, on the night He was betrayed, took bread, and when He had given thanks, He broke it and said, 'This is My body, which is for you; do this in remembrance of Me.' In the same way, after supper He took the cup, saying, 'This cup is the new covenant in My blood; do this, whenever you drink it, in remembrance of Me.' For whenever you eat this bread and drink this cup, you proclaim the Lord's death until He comes."]

I AM GOD OF SYMBOLS

Only show one to every player as each comes up—cover the rest!

1. Light

2. Star

3. Judge

4. Water

5. Rock

6. Door

7. Fountain

8. Fire

9. Oil (tiebreaker)

SESSION 3 | QUOTES AND VERSES

I AM GOD OF SYMBOLS

Exodus 13:21–22
"And the LORD went before them by day in a pillar of cloud to lead the way, and by night in a pillar of fire to give them light, so as to go by day and night. He did not take away the pillar of cloud by day or the pillar of fire by night from before the people."

1 John 1:5
"This is the message which we have heard from Him and declare to you, that God is light and in Him is no darkness at all."

Revelation 22:16
"I, Jesus, have sent My angel to testify to you these things in the churches. I am the Root and the Offspring of David, the Bright and Morning Star."

Psalm 75:6–7
"For exaltation comes neither from the east
Nor from the west nor from the south.
But God is the Judge:
He puts down one,
And exalts another."

John 4:14
"But whoever drinks of the water that I shall give him will never thirst. But the water that I shall give him will become in him a fountain of water springing up into everlasting life."

1 Corinthians 10:4
"For they drank of that spiritual Rock that followed them, and that Rock was Christ."

John 10:9
"I am the door. If anyone enters by Me, he will be saved, and will go in and out and find pasture."

Psalm 68:26
"Bless God in the congregations, the LORD, from the fountain of Israel."

Deuteronomy 4:24
"For the LORD your God is a consuming fire, a jealous God."

Leviticus 21:12
"For the consecration of the anointing oil of his God is upon him: I am the LORD."

God of Promise

WHAT YOU NEED

- One copy of the curriculum for the teacher
- Bibles
- One copy of the Quotes and Verses handout for each student
- Three copies of the Skit handouts for the teacher and two actors
- Prizes for the skit actors are always a good idea
- Pens or pencils for each student

RECOMMENDED READING

Teachers would greatly benefit from reading John Paul Jackson's two books *I AM: 365 Names of God* and *I AM: Inheriting the Fullness of God's Name*, both available from Streams Ministries (www.streamsministries.com or 1.888.441.8080). *I AM: 365 Names of God* is also available on a worship/meditation CD from Streams.

MULTIMEDIA IDEAS

 INTERNET

The website www.interviewwithgod.com/playprayer.htm features a beautiful animated version of The Lord's Prayer. The music does not fit with most teenagers' tastes, so we suggest showing the clip and playing a different song, such as the ones suggested below.

 VIDEO

Any film version of Jesus' life generally includes a scene of Him praying The Lord's Prayer. This could be shown.

 MUSIC

There are three powerful songs recorded on two CDs available from Streams Ministries (www.streamsministries.com or 1.888.441.8080):

"River Runs" (The Wildings) and "Raise It Up" (Chris Janzen) can both be found on the album *W2*, a Friends Langley Vineyard release. "River Runs" is a beautiful song full of the promise of God's love, while "Raise It Up" looks at the promise of God's influence.

"The Promise of Your Cross" by Matt Redman (on the album *Where Angels Fear to Tread*) is also very moving.

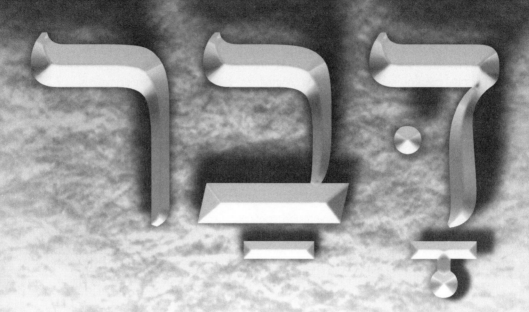

God of Promise

INTRODUCTION

Today, we are going to talk about God's promises. *Promise* is a word that gets used a lot.

—>> **What does the word *promise* mean to you?**

God is the God of Promise. He has made a covenant with His children, and He will deliver on what He has promised. Why? Because it is His name and His nature to do so.

THE IMPORTANCE OF GOD'S NAMES

God's name is the most powerful force in the universe, because it contains all His glory and acts. He isn't just God—He is God, Creator of Everything; God, Ruler of the World; God, Our Refuge. His names—all of them—tell us about who He truly is, because they describe His actions. The acts of God—healing, deliverance, peace, provision, love—are His name and His glory. His name, His acts, and His glory are inseparable.

——>> **Who can recite the Lord's Prayer?**

——>> **Who can tell me what *hallowed*, in the first line, means?**

The definition of *hallow* is "to revere, respect, value, cherish, and honor; to make holy or set apart for holy use." When Jesus taught us to pray by saying "hallowed be Your name," He meant that we need to recognize and esteem the full attributes of God.

Why is this important? When we pray "Our Father in heaven, hallowed be Your name," we are not simply honoring a single name for God. In this passage, the Greek word for "name" is plural: it means we are honoring every single combination of every possible name of God. Therefore, to hallow God's name means that we don't separate His name from His acts or His glory. We honor, revere, believe, and receive every aspect that His names express. We embrace the relevance, the nearness, and the accessibility of His names. We do not relegate them as names for different eras of time, such as a name for yesterday or a name for tomorrow. Instead, we inherit God's names—all of them—today.

God is not the God who used to do what His name depicts. No! He is the God who still does all that His name says.

If we don't get this, we're robbing ourselves of what God really wants for our lives. When we have difficulty embracing God's names, we have failed to believe and respond to all God says He is and does. We fail to experience everything that He really is, and the huge power of His glory.

In the Great Commission, Jesus released us to do all that He did *[have a student read Matthew 28:16–20 out loud: it's on their Quotes and Verses sheets]: "Then the eleven disciples went away into Galilee, to the mountain which Jesus had appointed for them. When they saw Him, they worshiped Him; but some doubted. And Jesus came and spoke to them, saying, 'All authority has been given to Me in heaven and on earth. Go therefore and make disciples of all the nations, baptizing them in the name of the Father and of the Son and of the Holy Spirit, teaching them to observe all things that I have commanded you; and lo, I am with you always, even to the end of the age.' Amen."*

As His followers, we are commanded to show others the names—and power—of God.

When we come to church, we should expect the wisdom and presence of God to be there. Healing, deliverance, salvation, peace, love, joy, wisdom, and all those attributes that exemplify the names of God should be present among believers, because they should be bearing God's name, and by extension, His glory and acts.

——>> Do you often feel God when you come to church?
Why or why not?

——>> What can you do to make your time with God better?

Nothing on earth is more important than bearing the name of God. Since His name is so precious, God will not carelessly give it away. Yet He offers it freely to any and all who want it and recognize what it means.

The prophet Malachi told of the joy God receives from those who honor His name. [*Have a student read Malachi 3:16 from their Quotes and Verses sheet*]: *"Then those who feared the LORD spoke to one another, and the LORD listened and heard them; So a book of remembrance was written before Him for those who fear the LORD and who meditate on His name."*

Close your eyes for a moment and picture God, sitting on His beautiful, massive throne in Heaven. Do you see Him there? Picture Him leaning back on His throne and listening to the conversations of those who fear and meditate on His name. Do you see how happy and content He is? He loves it so much He orders that a book be written in Heaven honoring those who so rightly honor Him.

Like a favorite DVD, God can look back at any instant to that book of remembrance and recall the pleasure of those men and women worshipping His name. "Read that to me again," He says to His angels and heavenly hosts. "I love that. One more time, please," He says. Do you see the pleasure He is receiving from Christians, like you and me, who are worshipping Him? We should hallow His name above all others.

——>> How will God remember your life?

——>> What dreams does He have for you?

——>> How many times has God written your name in His book of remembrance?

——>> How can you get it entered more often?

This is our number-one job on earth: to cherish and desire God's name more than anything or anyone else. Once we are convinced of the power and anointing contained in His names, we can then begin to act upon this assurance. The first step is simple—we must begin to learn and meditate on His names.

GOD OF PROMISE

One of the things God's names include is a number of promises to us. In the Bible, He put dozens of specific and powerful promises for us to hold Him to. God loves to be reminded of what He is going to do, because He gets glory for keeping His promises. Keeping promises is a key part of who God is.

This, of course, is very different from humans. We have problems keeping promises.
——>> Have you ever broken a promise?

>> **How does breaking your word feel?**

>> **Has someone ever broken a promise to you?**

>> **How did that feel?**

Promises, from God's perspective, can be taken to the bank—they are not *ifs*, they are concrete truths we can rely on.

SKIT

I have a couple of skits that may help explain this further. I need two volunteers, please.

CHARACTERS
God
A Person
The Narrator (*should be the group facilitator*)

SETTING
God and Person sit in two chairs, facing each other. The Narrator is among the group of students.

SKIT #1

Narrator (*loudly, as an introduction to the group*): It's easy for us to have distorted, incorrect views of who God is, because our insecurities stop us from really carrying God's name. This is how many of us perceive our relationship with God.

Person: Hi, God.

God: (*Yawn*) You again?

Person: Um, yeah. Me again. Anyway, I was thinking about the tough time I'm having at school.

God (*glancing at wristwatch*): Yeah, whatever.

Person: My friends and I aren't really getting along.

God (*trying to look past Person*): Would you move a bit? I'm missing what's on my heavenly TV.

Person (*looking sad*): Don't you have TiVo? Can't you tape it?

God (*angry*): Fine. Fine. I'm listening. I'm listening. (*Yawn*)

Person: Thanks. Now, as I was saying, my friends and I are having some problems.

God (*nods off to sleep*): Snore!

Person: What?!?

God: I said snore! As in, you're boring Me! Boring! Boring! Booooorrrrriiinnng! We talked about this before . . . I'm God—I don't forget! And I said I'd handle it when I got around to it!

Person: I can't believe You're saying this!

God: I can't believe you're wasting My time like this! I'm God, Master of the Universe!

Person: But . . .

God: I'm too busy for this.

(*God gets up and storms out.*)

CHARACTERS—SAME AS SKIT #1
God
A Person
The Narrator (*should be the group facilitator*)

SETTING—SAME AS SKIT #1
God and the Person sit in two chairs, facing each other. The Narrator is among the group of students.

SKIT #2

Narrator (*loudly, as an introduction to the group*): Obviously, that last skit was a little over the top. But here is a picture that is far closer to what really happens.

God: Hey, you! *Psssst!* You!

Person: Me?

God: Yeah, you! Did you know I love you more than anything? I want to give you everything your heart desires!

Person: What? Me? Are you sure you've got the right person?

God: Yeah, you! I know everything about you. I'm working for you, trying to make things better. Sorry about your friends—I know it hurts when people reject you.

Person: You do?

God: I do. I love you. I want to be everything for you—when things get rough, just ask Me for peace and kindness, and I'll give it to you!

Person: You would do that for me?

God: Of course! You're the most important thing in the world to Me! We can talk about this for as long as we need to. I want to be a part of your life.

Person: Really?

God: A long time ago, I told my buddy Jeremiah this: "I will bring health and healing; I will heal you and reveal to you lots of peace and truth." I'm God. This is what I do. I fulfill my promises to those who love Me. All you have to do is ask.

(*God and the person hug.*)

GOD OF PROMISE, PART TWO

Looking at these two skits, we see two very different views of God. The second is much closer to who He really is and wants to be for us. The problem is that we don't let Him fulfill His promises to us.

Let's look at a few of His promises. [*Have a student read John 14:3. It's on the Quotes and Verses handout*]: "And if I go and prepare a place for you, I will come again and receive you to Myself; that where I am, there you may be also."

——>> **What is included in this promise?**

——>> **What else did God promise Heaven will be like?**

This next promise is a bit stranger, but very cool, nonetheless. [*Have a student read Psalm 56:8; it's on the Quotes and Verses handout*]: "You number my wanderings; Put my tears into Your bottle; Are they not in Your book?"

——>> **What does this promise mean?**

——>> **Why would God care when we are sad?**

All right, let's look at a few more of God's promises, because they give us a deep look at who He wants to be for us. [*Have a student read John 16:13; it's on the Quotes and Verses handout*]: "However, when He, the Spirit of truth, has come, He will guide you into all truth; for He will not speak on His own authority, but whatever He hears He will speak; and He will tell you things to come."

——>> **This is a promise about the Holy Spirit. What do you think "all truth" means?**

——>> **Would you like to know "things to come"?**

——>> **Has God ever shown you something that hasn't happened yet?**

Here's a promise that should be at the front of every Christian's mind at all times. [*Have a student read Deuteronomy 4:29; it's on the Quotes and Verses handout*]: "But from there you will seek the Lord your God, and you will find Him if you seek Him with all your heart and with all your soul."

——>> **Have you ever sought God with all of your heart?**

One last promise to consider. *[Have a student read Numbers 12:6; it's on the Quotes and Verses handout]:* "If there is a prophet among you, I, the Lord, make Myself known to him in a vision; I speak to him in a dream."

——>> **Has God ever given you a dream?**

——>> **How did you know it was from Him?**

When you read the Bible, look at what God is promising you. Because He never changes, every blessing His name provides in the Bible is a promise you can take to the bank.

CONCLUSION

[Pray—perhaps for dreams or specific promises in each student's life—and dismiss them. One suggestion is to have them all picture themselves receiving a birthday present from God. What is in the box? Why did God give it to them? This can be a very powerful exercise—especially since teenagers learn visually. Picturing God interacting with them can be very helpful.]

SESSION 4 | QUOTES AND VERSES

I AM GOD OF PROMISE

Matthew 28:16–20
"Then the eleven disciples went away into Galilee, to the mountain which Jesus had appointed for them. When they saw Him, they worshiped Him; but some doubted. And Jesus came and spoke to them, saying, 'All authority has been given to Me in heaven and on earth. Go therefore and make disciples of all the nations, baptizing them in the name of the Father and of the Son and of the Holy Spirit, teaching them to observe all things that I have commanded you; and lo, I am with you always, even to the end of the age.' Amen."

Malachi 3:16
"Then those who feared the LORD spoke to one another, and the LORD listened and heard them; So a book of remembrance was written before Him for those who fear the LORD and who meditate on His name."

John 14:3
"And if I go and prepare a place for you, I will come again and receive you to Myself; that where I am, there you may be also."

Psalm 56:8
"You number my wanderings;
Put my tears into Your bottle;
Are they not in Your book?"

John 16:13
"However, when He, the Spirit of truth, has come, He will guide you into all truth; for He will not speak on His own authority, but whatever He hears He will speak; and He will tell you things to come."

Deuteronomy 4:29
"But from there you will seek the LORD your God, and you will find Him if you seek Him with all your heart and with all your soul."

Numbers 12:6
"If there is a prophet among you, I, the LORD, make Myself known to him in a vision; I speak to him in a dream."

SESSION 4 | SKIT #1

I AM GOD OF PROMISE

CHARACTERS
God
A Person
The Narrator (should be the group facilitator)

SETTING
God and the Person sit in two chairs, facing each other. Narrator is among the group of students.

SKIT #1

Narrator (*loudly, as an introduction to the group*): It's easy for us to have distorted, incorrect views of who God is, because our insecurities stop us from really carrying God's name. This is how many of us perceive our relationship with God.

Person: Hi, God.

God: (*Yawn*) You again?

Person: Um, yeah. Me again. Anyway, I was thinking about the tough time I'm having at school.

God (*glancing at wristwatch*)**:** Yeah, whatever.

Person: My friends and I aren't really getting along.

God (*trying to look past Person*)**:** Would you move a bit? I'm missing what's on my heavenly TV.

Person (*looking sad*)**:** Don't you have TiVo? Can't you tape it?

God (*angry*)**:** Fine. Fine. I'm listening. I'm listening. (*Yawn*)

Person: Thanks. Now, as I was saying, my friends and I are having some problems.

God (*nods off to sleep*)**:** *Snore!*

Person: What?!?

God: I said snore! As in, you're boring Me! Boring! Boring! Booooorrrrriiinnng! We talked about this before . . . I'm God—I don't forget! And I said I'd handle it when I got around to it!

Person: I can't believe You're saying this!

God: I can't believe you're wasting My time like this! I'm God, Master of the Universe!

Person: But . . .

God: I'm too busy for this.

(*God gets up and storms out.*)

CHARACTERS—SAME AS SKIT #1
God
A Person
The Narrator (*should be the group facilitator*)

SETTING—SAME AS SKIT #1
God and the Person sit in two chairs, facing each other. The Narrator is among the group of students.

SKIT #2

Narrator (*loudly, as an introduction to the group*): Obviously, that last skit was a little over the top. But here is a picture that is far closer to what really happens.

God: Hey, you! *Psssst!* You!

Person: Me?

God: Yeah, you! Did you know I love you more than anything? I want to give you everything your heart desires!

Person: What? Me? Are you sure you've got the right person?

God: Yeah, you! I know everything about you. I'm working for you, trying to make things better. Sorry about your friends—I know it hurts when people reject you.

Person: You do?

God: I do. I love you. I want to be everything for you—when things get rough, just ask Me for peace and kindness, and I'll give it to you!

Person: You would do that for me?

God: Of course! You're the most important thing in the world to Me! We can talk about this for as long as we need to. I want to be a part of your life.

Person: Really?

God: A long time ago, I told my buddy Jeremiah this: "I will bring health and healing; I will heal you and reveal to you lots of peace and truth." I'm God. This is what I do. I fulfill my promises to those who love Me. All you have to do is ask.

(*God and the person hug.*)

God the Shepherd

WHAT YOU NEED

- One copy of the curriculum for the teacher
- Bibles
- One copy of the Quotes and Verses handout for each student
- Enough copies of the small group exercises for everyone (you'll split the class into four small groups, and each group will be given a shepherd: Abel, Abraham, David, and Jesus' birth shepherds). Each group member needs a copy of the worksheet.
- Pens or pencils for each student

RECOMMENDED READING

Teachers would greatly benefit from reading John Paul Jackson's two books *I AM: 365 Names of God* and *I AM: Inheriting the Fullness of God's Name*, both available from Streams Ministries (www.streamsministries.com or 1.888.441.8080). *I AM: 365 Names of God* is also available on a worship/meditation CD from Streams.

MULTIMEDIA IDEAS

POWERPOINT

Pictures of shepherds and sheep would be a good visual aid. A good site to start looking for sheep photos is http://www.undiscoveredscotland.co.uk/uswallpaper/index.html. Performing a www.google.com image search for sheep is another idea.

VIDEO

Babe, the classic children's movie, features a hysterical scene of the little pig herding sheep at a big competition.

Visit your Sunday School the previous week with a video camera. Ask the three-and four-year olds to sing "Ba, Ba, Black Sheep." Film them. This is always good for a laugh as the kids get distracted, bored, fidgety, and hyper.

INTERNET

Psalm 23 is nicely captured in animation at www.interviewwithgod.com/psalm23.htm. We suggest replacing the music with the song below.

MUSIC

"Great Is the Lord's Love" by Melanie Thiessen is a beautiful recording found on the CD, *The Well: Live in the Spirit* from Friends Langley Vineyard, available from Streams Ministries (www.streamsministries.com or 1.888.441.8080).

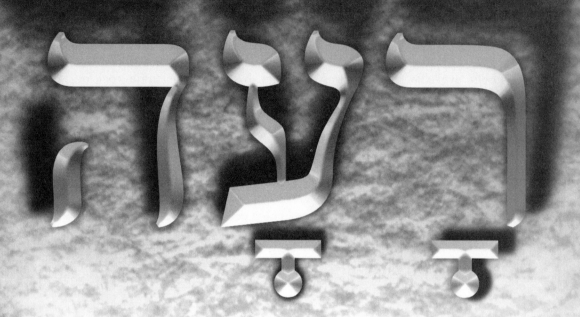

God the Shepherd

INTRODUCTION

This week, we're going to take a look at God the Shepherd. Shepherds have always been important in the Bible—they are everywhere!

—>> **Can anyone think of an example of a shepherd found in the Bible?**

—>> **Can anyone think of any other famous shepherds in TV, movies, or history?**

Later on today, we'll be talking about some different shepherds: Abel, Abraham, David, and the shepherds who attended Jesus' birth. First off, however, I just want to take a couple of minutes to talk about the importance of using God's names properly.

THE IMPORTANCE OF GOD'S NAMES

As we learn more about the names of God, we learn more about His nature. Nowhere is God revealed as powerfully or as clearly as in His names. When we know who God really is, we can be more like Him in every area of our lives.

Here is an example [*Get a student to read Proverbs 18:10 out loud; it's on their Quotes and Verses sheet*]: "The name of the LORD is a strong tower, The righteous run to it and are safe."

——>> **What does this verse mean?**

——>> **Has God ever protected you? Have you ever used God as a refuge from attack?**

——>> **How has He protected you in the past?**

Human language is incapable of putting all of God into a single name. God is so powerful, so wise, and so amazing, that no single name could ever come close to capturing the greatness of who He is and what He does. Because of this, to make Himself known to us, God used the Bible, which includes many names to describe Him. It is by these names that He is known today.

Unfortunately, many people have become so familiar with religious representations of God that His wonder and glory no longer hold any awe or mystery to them. Many have grown up being told that God is awesome and mighty, but they have not been able to figure out how carrying God's name should look in the personal realities of their every day lives. Our rote familiarity with His name has made us value it less. We say His name over and over: God, God, God, God, God, God, God, God, and it has become too normal for us. We must repent of that sin, ask Him to forgive us, and again fear and love and adore and revere the name of God.

——>> **Do you think you have God all figured out?**

——>> **What intrigues you about God?**

This is a piece of one of Moses' Ten Commandments [*Get a student to read Exodus 20:7; it's on their Quotes and Verses handout*]: "You shall not take the name of the LORD your God in vain, for the LORD will not hold him guiltless who takes His name in vain."

Grave consequences await those who misuse God's name. His name has been used wrongly in magic, in swearing, and in cursing. It has even been misused in court by people who lie after swearing on His name.

——>> **Have you ever misused God's name? How did you feel afterward?**

——>> **How do you feel when you're around someone who takes the Lord's name in vain?**

By speaking God's name, the Israelites understood that awesome and awful power would be released against God's enemies, that miracles would occur, and that He would appear. God's name was like none other, a name deserving the utmost honor, reverence, and respect. His name, above all others, deserved to be hallowed.

Although He wants us to treat Him with a holy fear, God doesn't want us to be afraid of His name. In fact, He wants us to call out His name so that it can become a shield of protection and a place of blessing for us. God wants to give us His name. He calls us His children, and all children have the names of their parents. To be called His child is a sign of great love.

——>> **What does it mean to be a child of God?**

——>> **Have you ever desperately called on the name of God to save you? What happened?**

God wants to put His name on us, but He will only do so with those who have learned to rightly carry it.

GOD THE SHEPHERD

Let's switch gears a bit and look at what it means when we say God is a Shepherd. It was Jesus who really popularized this name for God [*Have a student read John 10:14; it's on their Quotes and Verses handout*]: "I am the good shepherd; and I know My sheep, and am known by My own."

Being a shepherd wasn't a fancy job to have in those days; it was stinky and difficult. You spent hours and hours and hours outside, day and night, making sure your sheep were okay. You had to fight off lions, bears, wolves, foxes, and thieves, and you were usually a long way from home. Plus, sheep are dumb. Has anyone seen the movie *Babe*? In that movie the sheep wander and seem confused until the little pig tells them what to do. Sheep are stubborn and often wander off.

——>> **If being a shepherd was so bad, why did Jesus call Himself the Good Shepherd?**

——>> **How are we like sheep?**

Jesus' Good Shepherd speech was a tribute to a song King David had written several centuries before, Psalm 23. In Psalm 23, we learn more about what God the Shepherd is like. Let's read it out loud [*Have a student read verse 1, then another student verse 2, and so on; it's on their Quotes and Verses handout*]:

1 "The Lord is my shepherd;
I shall not want.

2 He makes me to lie down in green pastures;
He leads me beside the still waters.

3 He restores my soul;
He leads me in the paths of righteousness
For His name's sake.

4 Yea, though I walk through the valley of the shadow of death,
   I will fear no evil;
   For You are with me;
   Your rod and Your staff, they comfort me.

5 You prepare a table before me in the presence of my enemies;
   You anoint my head with oil;
   My cup runs over.

6 Surely goodness and mercy shall follow me
   All the days of my life;
   And I will dwell in the house of the Lord
   Forever."

>> **What can we learn about God's nature in this psalm? Let's list some of the attributes God shows us about Himself.**

>> **What stands out in this psalm for you?**

God called Himself a shepherd because it's a great picture of how He cares for you and me. He leads us to eat and drink, He keeps us safe from the enemy, He comforts us. When we're scared to death, He is our protection. What an amazing gift!

There are many shepherds in the Bible, some of whom give us an even better picture of what God the Shepherd is like.

SMALL GROUP EXERCISE

[Split the class into four groups. Give each group one set of sheets—Group 1: Abel; Group 2: Abraham; Group 3: Jesus' birth shepherds; and Group 4: David. Have each group work through the sheets together. Allow between ten and twenty minutes. Circulate, and encourage the groups not to settle for pat answers but to dig deep into what the Bible is saying.]

SESSION 5—SMALL GROUP: 1 (ABEL)
I AM GOD THE SHEPHERD

A. Read the following verses.

Genesis 4:2–6
"Now, Abel was a keeper of sheep, but Cain was a tiller of the ground. And in the process of time it came to pass that Cain brought an offering of the fruit of the ground to the LORD. Abel also brought of the firstborn of his flock and of their fat. And the Lord respected Abel and his offering, but He did not respect Cain and his offering. And Cain was very angry, and his countenance fell. So the LORD said to Cain, 'Why are you angry? And why has your countenance fallen? If you do well, will you not be accepted? And if you do not do well, sin lies at the door. And its desire is for you, but you should rule over it.'

Hebrews 11:4
"By faith Abel offered to God a more excellent sacrifice than Cain, through which he obtained witness that he was righteous, God testifying of his gifts; and through it he being dead still speaks."

B. Discuss and answer the following questions.

    1. Why did God respect Abel's sacrifice and not Cain's?

    2. What do you think it means to have God "testify" of our gifts?

    3. What does the story of Cain and Abel tell you about God the Shepherd?

    4. In worship, who are we more like—Abel, whose sacrifice depended on what God wanted, or Cain, whose sacrifice depended on how he himself felt?

    5. Who would you rather be in life—an Abel motivated by love for God, or a Cain, full of anger? How can we become more like Abel?

SESSION 5—SMALL GROUP: 2 (ABRAHAM)
I AM GOD THE SHEPHERD

A. Read the following verses.

Genesis 13:2, NIV
"Abram had become very wealthy in livestock and in silver and gold."

Genesis 15:1, 5–6, NIV
After this, the word of the LORD came to Abram in a vision: "Do not be afraid, Abram. I am your shield, your very great reward." He took him outside and said, "Look up at the heavens and count the stars—if indeed you can count them." Then he said to him, "So shall your offspring be." Abram believed the LORD, and he credited it to him as righteousness.

James 2:23
"And the Scripture was fulfilled which says, 'Abraham believed God, and it was accounted to him for righteousness.' And he was called the friend of God."

Hebrews 11:8
"By faith Abraham obeyed when he was called to go out to the place which he would receive as an inheritance. And he went out, not knowing where he was going."

B. Discuss and answer the following questions.

    1. Why was it important for Abraham to realize that God was his shield and reward?

    2. Do you think you could be considered a "friend of God"?

    3. What does the story of Abraham tell you about God the Shepherd?

    4. The Bible says, "Abraham believed God, and it was credited to him as righteousness." What has God promised you that, if you would believe it, would be credited to you as righteousness?

SESSION 5—SMALL GROUP: 3 (JESUS' BIRTH)
I AM GOD THE SHEPHERD

A. Read the following verses.

Luke 2:8–20
"Now there were in the same country shepherds living out in the fields, keeping watch over their flock by night. And behold, an angel of the Lord stood before them, and the glory of the Lord shone around them, and they were greatly afraid. Then the angel said to them, 'Do not be afraid, for behold, I bring you good tidings of great joy which will be to all people. For there is born to you this day in the city of David a Savior, who is Christ the Lord. And this will be the sign to you: You will find a Babe wrapped in swaddling cloths, lying in a manger.' And suddenly there was with the angel a multitude of the heavenly host praising God and saying: 'Glory to God in the highest, and on earth peace, goodwill toward men!'

So it was, when the angels had gone away from them into heaven, that the shepherds said to one another, 'Let us now go to Bethlehem and see this thing that has come to pass, which the Lord has made known to us.' And they came with haste and found Mary and Joseph, and the Babe lying in a manger. Now when they had seen Him, they made widely known the saying which was told them concerning this Child. And all those who heard it marveled at those things which were told them by the shepherds. But Mary kept all these things and pondered them in her heart. Then the shepherds returned, glorifying and praising God for all the things that they had heard and seen, as it was told them."

B. Discuss and answer the following questions.

1. How important are these shepherds in the Christmas story? Why or why not?

2. The Bible says, "Now, when they had seen Him, they made widely known the saying which was told them concerning this Child." If you had an experience like the shepherds, would it affect what you tell people about Jesus? How?

3. What does the story of these shepherds tell you about God the Shepherd?

4. Why do you think God chose these shepherds to share the good news with? Why not a prince or businessman or priest?

SESSION 5—SMALL GROUP: 4 (DAVID)
I AM GOD THE SHEPHERD

A. Read the following verses.

1 Samuel 16:11–13
"And Samuel said to Jesse, 'Are all the young men here?' Then he said, 'There remains yet the youngest, and there he is, keeping the sheep.' And Samuel said to Jesse, 'Send and bring him. For we will not sit down till he comes here.' So he sent and brought him in. Now he was ruddy, with bright eyes, and good-looking. And the LORD said, 'Arise, anoint him; for this is the one!' Then Samuel took the horn of oil and anointed him in the midst of his brothers; and the Spirit of the LORD came upon David from that day forward. So Samuel arose and went to Ramah."

1 Samuel 17:34–37

"But David said to Saul, 'Your servant used to keep his father's sheep, and when a lion or a bear came and took a lamb out of the flock, I went out after it and struck it, and delivered the lamb from its mouth; and when it arose against me, I caught it by its beard, and struck and killed it. Your servant has killed both lion and bear; and this uncircumcised Philistine will be like one of them, seeing he has defied the armies of the living God.' Moreover David said, 'The LORD, who delivered me from the paw of the lion and from the paw of the bear, He will deliver me from the hand of this Philistine.' And Saul said to David, 'Go, and the LORD be with you!'"

B. Discuss and answer the following questions.

1. David had confidence to kill Goliath in public because he had killed lions and bears in private. How can this idea be applied to our spiritual lives?

2. David seemed to put more trust in God to defeat Goliath than in his own talents. Do you agree with this statement? Why or why not?

3. What does the story of David tell you about God the Shepherd?

4. The Bible calls David a person "after God's own heart." Would this description fit your life? Would you like it to? Why or why not?

SMALL GROUP EXERCISE OUTFLOW

[If there is time, have the groups read their stories and answers out loud. Feel free to add to them, or encourage more discussion on them. The key to this stuff isn't a right or wrong answer, but a good, open dialogue.]

CONCLUSION

[Pray—asking one of the students, perhaps—and dismiss]

I AM GOD THE SHEPHERD

Proverbs 18:10
"The name of the LORD is a strong tower,
The righteous run to it and are safe."

Exodus 20:7
"You shall not take the name of the Lord your God in vain, for the Lord will not hold him guiltless who takes His name in vain."

John 10:14
"I am the good shepherd; and I know My sheep, and am known by My own."

Psalm 23
1 "The Lord is my shepherd;
   I shall not want.

2 He makes me to lie down in green pastures;
   He leads me beside the still waters.

3 He restores my soul;
   He leads me in the paths of righteousness
   For His name's sake.

4 Yea, though I walk through the valley of the shadow of death,
   I will fear no evil;
   For You are with me;
   Your rod and Your staff, they comfort me.

5 You prepare a table before me in the presence of my enemies;
   You anoint my head with oil;
   My cup runs over.

6 Surely goodness and mercy shall follow me
   All the days of my life;
   And I will dwell in the house of the Lord
   Forever."

SESSION 5 | SMALL GROUP: 1 (ABEL)

I AM GOD THE SHEPHERD

A. Read the following verses.

Genesis 4:2–6
"Now Abel was a keeper of sheep, but Cain was a tiller of the ground. And in the process of time it came to pass that Cain brought an offering of the fruit of the ground to the LORD. Abel also brought of the firstborn of his flock and of their fat. And the LORD respected Abel and his offering, but He did not respect Cain and his offering. And Cain was very angry, and his countenance fell. So the LORD said to Cain, 'Why are you angry? And why has your countenance fallen? If you do well, will you not be accepted? And if you do not do well, sin lies at the door. And its desire is for you, but you should rule over it.'"

Hebrews 11:4
By faith Abel offered to God a more excellent sacrifice than Cain, through which he obtained witness that he was righteous, God testifying of his gifts; and through it he being dead still speaks.

B. Discuss and answer the following questions.

1. Why did God respect Abel's sacrifice and not Cain's?

2. What do you think it means to have God "testify" of our gifts?

3. What does the story of Cain and Abel tell you about God the Shepherd?

4. In worship, who are we more like—Abel, whose sacrifice depended on what God wanted, or Cain, whose sacrifice depended on how he himself felt?

5. Who would you rather be in life—an Abel motivated by love for God, or a Cain, full of anger? How can we become more like Abel?

SESSION 5 | SMALL GROUP: 2 (ABRAHAM)

I AM GOD THE SHEPHERD

A. Read the following verses.

Genesis 13:2, NIV
"Abram had become very wealthy in livestock and in silver and gold."

Genesis 15:1, 5–6, NIV
After this, the word of the LORD came to Abram in a vision: "Do not be afraid, Abram. I am your shield, your very great reward." He took him outside and said, "Look up at the heavens and count the stars—if indeed you can count them." Then he said to him, "So shall your offspring be." Abram believed the LORD, and he credited it to him as righteousness.

James 2:23
"And the Scripture was fulfilled which says, 'Abraham believed God, and it was accounted to him for righteousness.' And he was called the friend of God."

Hebrews 11:8
"By faith Abraham obeyed when he was called to go out to the place which he would receive as an inheritance. And he went out, not knowing where he was going."

B. Discuss and answer the following questions.

1. Why was it important for Abraham to realize that God was his shield and reward?

2. Do you think you could be considered a "friend of God"?

3. What does the story of Abraham tell you about God the Shepherd?

4. The Bible says, "Abram believed the Lord, and He credited it to him as righteousness." What has God promised you that, if you would believe it, would be credited to you as righteousness?

I AM GOD THE SHEPHERD

A. Read the following verses.

Luke 2:8–20
"Now there were in the same country shepherds living out in the fields, keeping watch over their flock by night. And behold, an angel of the Lord stood before them, and the glory of the Lord shone around them, and they were greatly afraid. Then the angel said to them, 'Do not be afraid, for behold, I bring you good tidings of great joy which will be to all people. For there is born to you this day in the city of David a Savior, who is Christ the Lord. And this will be the sign to you: You will find a Babe wrapped in swaddling cloths, lying in a manger.' And suddenly there was with the angel a multitude of the heavenly host praising God and saying: 'Glory to God in the highest, and on earth peace, goodwill toward men!'

So it was, when the angels had gone away from them into heaven, that the shepherds said to one another, 'Let us now go to Bethlehem and see this thing that has come to pass, which the Lord has made known to us.' And they came with haste and found Mary and Joseph, and the Babe lying in a manger. Now when they had seen Him, they made widely known the saying which was told them concerning this Child. And all those who heard it marveled at those things which were told them by the shepherds. But Mary kept all these things and pondered them in her heart. Then the shepherds returned, glorifying and praising God for all the things that they had heard and seen, as it was told them."

B. Discuss and answer the following questions.

1. How important are these shepherds in the Christmas story? Why or why not?

2. The Bible says, "Now when they had seen Him, they made widely known the saying which was told them concerning this Child." If you had an experience like theirs, how would you tell people about Jesus?

3. What does the story of these shepherds tell you about God the Shepherd?

4. Why do you think God chose to share the good news with these shepherds? Why not a prince or businessman or priest?

I AM GOD THE SHEPHERD

A. Read the following verses.

1 Samuel 16:11–13
"And Samuel said to Jesse, 'Are all the young men here?' Then he said, 'There remains yet the youngest, and there he is, keeping the sheep.' And Samuel said to Jesse, 'Send and bring him. For we will not sit down till he comes here.' So he sent and brought him in. Now he was ruddy, with bright eyes, and good-looking. And the LORD said, 'Arise, anoint him; for this is the one!' Then Samuel took the horn of oil and anointed him in the midst of his brothers; and the Spirit of the LORD came upon David from that day forward. So Samuel arose and went to Ramah."

1 Samuel 17:34–37
"But David said to Saul, 'Your servant used to keep his father's sheep, and when a lion or a bear came and took a lamb out of the flock, I went out after it and struck it, and delivered the lamb from its mouth; and when it arose against me, I caught it by its beard, and struck and killed it. Your servant has killed both lion and bear; and this uncircumcised Philistine will be like one of them, seeing he has defied the armies of the living God.' Moreover David said, 'The LORD, who delivered me from the paw of the lion and from the paw of the bear, He will deliver me from the hand of this Philistine.' And Saul said to David, 'Go, and the LORD be with you!'"

B. Discuss and answer the following questions.

1. David had confidence to kill Goliath in public because he had killed lions and bears in private. How can this idea be applied to our spiritual lives?

2. David seemed to put more trust in God to defeat Goliath than in his own talents. Do you agree with this statement? Why or why not?

3. What does the story of David tell you about God the Shepherd?

4. The Bible calls David a person "after God's own heart." Would this description fit your life? Would you like it to? Why or why not?

WHAT YOU NEED

- One copy of the curriculum for the teacher
- Bibles
- Enough copies of the Quotes and Verses handout for everyone.
- Pens or pencils for each student
- Three copies of the Skit handout
- One red pill and one blue pill (candy, of course) for the Skit (and, if you have them, two pairs of wraparound sunglasses)
- A bowl full of red pills (red M&Ms)—enough for everyone

RECOMMENDED READING

Teachers would greatly benefit from reading John Paul Jackson's two books *I AM: 365 Names of God* and *I AM: Inheriting the Fullness of God's Name*, both available from Streams Ministries (www.streamsministries.com or 1.888.441.8080). *I AM: 365 Names of God* is also available on a worship/meditation CD from Streams.

MULTIMEDIA IDEAS

POWERPOINT
A simple graphic of a red pill and a blue pill would work as a solid PowerPoint presentation.

VIDEO
Gladiator, the Oscar-winning Russell Crowe movie, has a powerful scene in which Maximus yells, "What you do in life echoes in eternity!" This speech might be worth showing.

Braveheart, the Oscar-winning Mel Gibson movie, has a similarly powerful scene in which William Wallace says, "Every man dies. But not every man really lives." This speech might be worth showing as well.

The Matrix (the original film, not the two sequels) contains a scene where Morpheus offers Neo a choice: the blue pill or the red pill. One would shift Neo's view of the world forever, allowing him to enter his destiny. The other would rob him of that call. This is a magnificent scene and the foundation for the second part of this session. A skit with this dialogue is included; a good idea might be to show the movie clip at the beginning of your time together and to use the skit later on.

INTERNET
A great graphic to have running during your session is the Matrix falling computer code. It is available as a screensaver download at http://www.home-pagez.com/grantsmatrix/matrix.zip or at http://www.3d-screensaver-download.com/matrixworld3d_ts.exe.

MUSIC
"It's Time" by The Wildings can be found on the Wilding's *Wide-Eyed Wonder,* available from Streams Ministries (www.streamsministries.com or 1.888.441.8080).

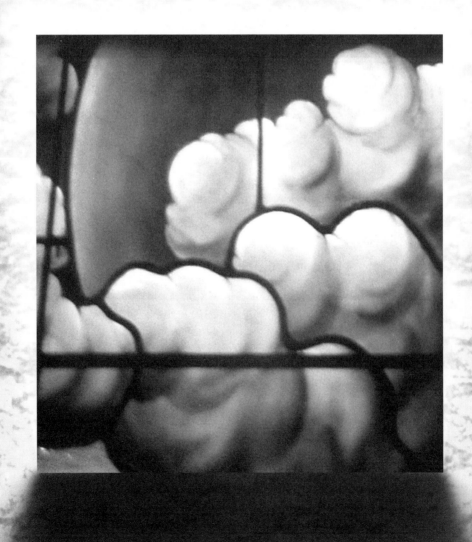

God of Eternity

INTRODUCTION

This week we're going to take a look at God and eternity. The Bible is full of references to the timelessness of God. This, of course, is hard for us to imagine, because we are bound by the constraints of time. Time is all we know.

——>> Close your eyes, and imagine eternity: an endless stretch of time—year after year, decade after decade, century after century. Time simply ceases to exist. What comes to your mind? How does it make you feel?

——>> What would it be like to live in a world without time? Can you imagine such a place?

Why is it important for us to ponder such things? [*Have a student read Hebrews 13:8 aloud; it's on the Quotes and Verses sheet*]: "Jesus Christ is the same yesterday, today and forever." Later on we'll look more at God's role in eternity and the conflict time presents.

THE IMPORTANCE OF GOD'S NAMES

First, however, let us examine briefly the importance of the names of God in our lives. Through our studies over the past several sessions we have seen the power contained in God's names. But it's not enough to simply know His names—we must learn how to call on them and make them a part of our daily lives. God has many blessings to give us, and we can ask Him for them. As we learn more about what it means to carry the names of God into real life, we can apply that power when situations are tough. Sometimes life stinks. Things come against us: we have a rough time at school, in friendships, in life. But God's names can protect and help us— they really can. And the more we rely on God's help, the more like Him we become.

> ——>> Privately, with your eyes closed, think of the problems you are facing right now in your life. What is weighing you down?

> ——>> Now ask yourself this: Could God be teaching me something about His relationship with me through this issue?

When our problems are pressing in on us, Christians have two choices. The first is to look at those issues and feel anxious, afraid, and worried. In a way we end up agreeing that we're in deep trouble.

The second choice—God's choice—is to look instead at what Jesus is doing and to ask Him for His help. If we feel lonely, could it be that God wants to draw us closer to Him? If we feel scared, could He want to be our safety? If we're sick, perhaps He wants to heal us? We have the ability to call on Jesus when things are grim and ask Him to use the power of His names to help us. We can draw strength and faith from His names, and from the beautiful character and promises contained within them. Whatever our need, and whatever our weakness, we can always find our answer and hope in one of His names. Do we need peace? Do we need love? Do we need direction? It's all contained within His names.

When we are tested, we must learn to rely on the truth of His names. Only there will we find our needs met. *[Have a student read Psalm 116:4–5 out loud; it's in the Quotes and Verses sheet]*: "Then I called upon the name of the LORD: 'O LORD, I implore You, deliver my soul!' Gracious is the LORD, and righteous; Yes, our God is merciful."

> ——>> Again, close your eyes. Privately ask yourself this question: What aspect of God's name and nature would help you most in the problem you currently face? Now ask God to give you that part of Him.

The Bible says that every good and perfect gift comes from God. He loves you more than you can ever imagine or dream. He wants you to be happy. He wants you to be strong. He wants you to be kind. He wants you to be fun. He wants you to be compassionate. Why does He want you to be all of these good things? Because He is all of these things! He wants you to be to others what He is to you!

> ——>> What do you love about God?

——>> Could we learn to be that way with others?

If we are judgmental and bitter, we should stop and look at how we think God is. It is most likely that we have fallen into a trap of believing He is judgmental and bitter with us. Nothing could be further from the truth! You make God's heart leap with joy. When He sees you, He grins. He loves you more than your best friend, parents, girlfriend, youth pastor, and everyone else on earth put together ever could. His heart is full of good things for you: all you have to do is ask Him for them.

GOD OF ETERNITY

Earlier on we talked about how God is the God of Eternity.

——>> Who can define the word *eternity*?

——>> What does it mean when we say God is *eternal*?

Eternity is a difficult concept for us to understand. Yet God created everything—even time! In Psalm 90:2 God is called everlasting [*Have a student read Psalm 90:2; it's on the Quotes and Verses handout*]: "Before the mountains were brought forth, or ever You had formed the earth and the world, even from everlasting to everlasting, You are God."

The Bible is full of references to the timelessness of God. Let's look at a few of these verses. [*Have a student read Psalm 10:16; it's on the Quotes and Verses handout*]: "The LORD is King forever and ever; the nations have perished out of His land."

——>> Has anyone heard of the terms *Alpha and Omega*?
          What do you think that means?

Let's look at the verse that it comes from: [*Have a student read Revelation 22:13; it's on the Quotes and Verses handout*]: "I am the Alpha and Omega, the Beginning and the End, the First and the Last." Alpha is the first and Omega is the last of the letters in the Greek alphabet. In our language, Alpha and Omega would translate as *A* and *Z*. God first, God last. God all the time. God outside of time. Amazing, eh?

We may find it hard to understand eternity because our minds are always so focused on the issue of time. Yet God exists outside of time. Imagine time as a shoebox in your hands. The past, present, and future all exist inside that box. But you represent God: you are outside that box! God makes the issue of time seem insignificant.

A great movie that can help us understand this idea a little more is *The Matrix*. In it two characters, Neo and Morpheus, have a discussion about the Matrix humanity is trapped in. Let's have two people reenact that scene. May I have two volunteers please [*set up for Skit*]?

I AM GOD OF ETERNITY

CHARACTERS
Neo
Morpheus
The Narrator (*should be the group facilitator*)

SETTING
Neo and Morpheus sit in two chairs, facing each other. Morpheus has a "red pill" and a "blue pill." The Narrator is among the group of students.

SKIT

Narrator (*loudly, as an introduction to the group*)**:** As you listen to this conversation, try to imagine that the Matrix Morpheus refers to is time-based, everyday life without an understanding of the power of the God of Eternity.

Morpheus: At last. Welcome, Neo. As you've no doubt guessed, I am Morpheus.

Neo: It's an honor to meet you.

Morpheus: No, the honor is mine. Please, come. Sit. I imagine that right now you're feeling a bit like Alice tumbling down the rabbit hole, hmm?

Neo: You might say that.

Morpheus: I can see it in your eyes. You have the look of a man who accepts what he sees because he is expecting to wake up. Ironically this is not far from the truth. Do you believe in fate, Neo?

Neo: No.

Morpheus: Why not?

Neo: Because I don't like the idea that I'm not in control of my life.

Morpheus: I know exactly what you mean. Let me tell you why you're here. You're here because you know something. What you know you can't explain. But you feel it. You've felt it your entire life. You've felt there's something wrong with the world. You don't know what it is, but it's there, like a splinter in your mind driving you mad. It's this feeling that has brought you to me. Do you know what I'm talking about?

Neo: The Matrix?

Morpheus: Do you want to know what it is? The Matrix is everywhere. It's all around us, even now in this very room. You can see it when you look out your window or when you turn on your television. You can feel it when you go to work, when you go to church, when you pay your taxes. It's the world that's been pulled over your eyes to blind you from the truth.

Neo: What truth?

Morpheus: That you're a slave, Neo. Like everyone else, you were born into bondage, born into a prison you cannot smell or taste or touch. A prison for your mind. Unfortunately no one can be told what the Matrix is. You have to see it for yourself. This is your last chance. After this there's no turning back. You take the blue pill, the story ends, you wake up in your bed and believe whatever you want to believe. You take the red pill, you stay in Wonderland, and I show you how deep the rabbit hole goes. Remember, all I'm offering is the truth, nothing more.

Neo takes the red pill, and the two stand up and walk out together.

[Thunderous applause.]

——>> What strikes you about the conversation between Neo and Morpheus?

Neo obviously took the red pill: he wanted to know the truth about his existence. That same choice is offered to us by God every day. Do we want to take the blue pill and just live our timedriven life, scraping by according to the matrix of the world? Or do we want to see clearly, taking the red pill, and understanding more of how God perceives the world?

Like the matrix, time is everywhere. It's all around us. It's unavoidable. Morpheus told Neo that the matrix "has been pulled over our eyes to blind us from the truth. Like everyone else, we were born into bondage, born into a prison that we cannot smell or taste or touch." But God has called us to carry the timelessness of His name. We are eternal beings having a temporary time-driven experience. Christians have the ability to live an eternal life—to follow God long after time ceases to exist. We need to find a way out of the shoebox, out of the matrix, and into the timelessness of God.

The way to do this is to thank God for holding eternity in His hands. If we could just see the world as God sees it, everything would change.

——>> How do you think an eternal God sees the world?

——>> What do you think God thinks of time?

The concept of time clouds our vision of God. If we could see eternally as He does, a lot of the issues and problems in our lives would seem unimportant. We would be able to grasp the freedom that comes with knowing things always work themselves out. Isaiah 46:10 records the promise of God to us [*Have a student read Isaiah 46:10; it's on the Quotes and Verses handout*]: "Declaring the end from the beginning, and from ancient times things that are not yet done, saying, 'My counsel shall stand, and I will do all My pleasure.'"

——>> If you knew how your life would play out, how would that change the way you deal with hard situations?

God has a plan for each of us that is greater than we could ever dream or imagine. Just as eternity is beyond our mind's ability to comprehend, so is His love for us. Our job is to trust Him, to reject the blue pill of the matrix of time, and take His red pill of eternal life.

CONCLUSION

[*Show kids the bowl of red M&Ms; ask them to take some as a sign to God that they want the red pill of His freedom. Pray.*]

I AM GOD OF ETERNITY

CHARACTERS

Neo

Morpheus

The Narrator (*should be the group facilitator*)

SETTING

Neo and Morpheus sit in two chairs, facing one another. Morpheus has a "red pill" and a "blue pill." Narrator is among the group of students.

SKIT

Narrator (*loudly, as an introduction to the group*): As you listen to this conversation, try to imagine that the Matrix Morpheus refers to is time-based, everyday life without an understanding of the power of the God of Eternity.

Morpheus: At last. Welcome, Neo. As you've no doubt guessed, I am Morpheus.

Neo: It's an honor to meet you.

Morpheus: No, the honor is mine. Please, come. Sit. I imagine that right now you're feeling a bit like Alice tumbling down the rabbit hole, hmm?

Neo: You might say that.

Morpheus: I can see it in your eyes. You have the look of a man who accepts what he sees because he is expecting to wake up. Ironically this is not far from the truth. Do you believe in fate, Neo?

Neo: No.

Morpheus: Why not?

Neo: Because I don't like the idea that I'm not in control of my life.

Morpheus: I know exactly what you mean. Let me tell you why you're here. You're here because you know something. What you know you can't explain. But you feel it. You've felt it your entire life. You've felt there's something wrong with the world. You don't know what it is, but it's there, like a splinter in your mind driving you mad. It's this feeling that has brought you to me. Do you know what I'm talking about?

Neo: The Matrix?

Morpheus: Do you want to know what it is? The Matrix is everywhere. It's all around us, even now in this very room. You can see it when you look out your window or when you turn on your television. You can feel it when you go to work, when you go to church, when you pay your taxes. It's the world that's been pulled over your eyes to blind you from the truth.

Neo: What truth?

Morpheus: That you're a slave, Neo. Like everyone else, you were born into bondage, born into a prison you cannot smell or taste or touch. A prison for your mind. Unfortunately no one can be told what the Matrix is. You have to see it for yourself. This is your last chance. After this there's no turning back. You take the blue pill, the story ends, you wake up in your bed and believe whatever you want to believe. You take the red pill, you stay in Wonderland, and I show you how deep the rabbit hole goes. Remember, all I'm offering is the truth, nothing more.

Neo takes the red pill, and the two stand up and walk out together.

[Thunderous applause.]

I AM GOD OF ETERNITY

Hebrews 13:8
"Jesus Christ is the same yesterday, today, and forever."

Psalm 116:4–5
"Then I called upon the name of the LORD: 'O LORD, I implore You, deliver my soul!' Gracious is the LORD, and righteous; Yes, our God is merciful."

Psalm 90:2
"Before the mountains were brought forth, or ever You had formed the earth and the world, even from everlasting to everlasting, You are God."

Psalm 10:16
"The LORD is King forever and ever; the nations have perished out of His land."

Revelation 22:13
"I am the Alpha and the Omega, the Beginning and the End, the First and the Last."

Isaiah 46:10
"Declaring the end from the beginning, and from ancient times things that are not yet done, saying, 'My counsel shall stand, and I will do all My pleasure.'"

God of Sacrifice

WHAT YOU NEED

- One copy of the curriculum for the teacher
- Bibles
- Enough copies of the Quotes and Verses handout for everyone
- Pens or pencils for each student
- Enough copies of the Rosary handout for everyone

RECOMMENDED READING

Teachers would greatly benefit from reading John Paul Jackson's two books *I AM: 365 Names of God* and *I AM: Inheriting the Fullness of God's Name,* both available from Streams Ministries (www.streamsministries.com or 1.888.441.8080). *I AM: 365 Names of God* is also available on a worship/meditation CD from Streams.

MULTIMEDIA IDEAS

VIDEO

Any depiction of the crucifixion of Christ would fit with this presentation. Use your discretion regarding what might fit best with your students. The world-renowned *Jesus* video is a safe bet.

COMPUTER ANIMATION

A California-based ministry called Highway Video produces high-quality, trendy animations for church groups. If you log on to www.highwayvideo.com and purchase their *VIBE Videos, Vol. 4,* you will receive five great presentations that can be used throughout this twelve-week course. For this week's class we suggest showing "Potter," which features a video of a potter making a clay pot, and firing it in a kiln.

INTERNET

A beautiful computer presentation (complete with Scripture and prophecy) of the Way of the Cross, an ancient meditation on Christ's sacrifice, is available at http://www.beliefnet.com/religion/christianity/holyweek/easter/cross_lite2.html.

The Vertical Horizon song "Everything I Want" is used to augment a video of Christ's crucifixion. You can download it at http://emergingminister.com/video/vertical.mpg.

Seven meditations on Jesus' seven sayings on the cross can be found at http://www.rejesus.co.uk/spirituality/seven_sayings/index.html.

MUSIC

"Blessed Be Your Name," a song from Matt Redman's album *Where Angels Fear to Tread,* is an amazing song of serving God in the midst of sacrifice. Another fantastic song on the same CD is "The Promise of Your Cross." You can order the album from Streams Ministries at 1.888.441.8080 or online at www.streamsministries.com.

Worship Together offers a compilation of twelve beautiful worship songs, all focusing on the cross, on the album *The Wonderful Cross.* Matt Redman, Tim Hughes, Rebecca St. James and others are featured on the CD.

זכה

God of Sacrifice

INTRODUCTION

Today we're going to look at Jesus, who sacrificed every-thing—even His own life—for us. Sacrifice is one of those themes Christians don't like to talk about.

>>> **When I mention the word *sacrifice*, what images come to mind?**

Sacrifice flies in the face of our culture. From a young age we're taught to take and get as much as we can. Being generous becomes a difficult task for us. Yet we must understand what it means to sacrifice in order to truly understand the love of God.

THE IMPORTANCE OF GOD'S NAMES

First, however, let's continue to examine the importance of the names of God in our lives. God is looking far and wide for those whom He can trust to carry His names, who won't be corrupted by the blessings they will bring. He loves us too much to give His name to us before we are ready, because He knows we will be tempted to abuse and misuse them, and then He'll be forced to pour out His judgment on us.

God loves us too much to put us in a situation that is more than we can handle, as Paul explained in 1 Corinthians 10:13 [*Have a student read 1 Corinthians 10:13; it's on the Quotes and Verses handout*]: "No temptation has overtaken you except such as is common to man; but God is faithful, who will not allow you to be tempted beyond what you are able, but with the temptation will also make the way of escape, that you may be able to bear it."

——>> **Have you ever truly been tempted beyond what you could bear?**

——>> **Why does God make us this promise in 1 Corinthians 10:13?**

The Bible makes it clear that all of us will be judged for how we treat God's name. Therefore God will not give us His name when He knows He will have to judge us harshly for it later. He will reserve His name and the blessings it brings for those with the character and humility to carry it properly. As in Isaiah 30:18 [*Have a student read Isaiah 30:18; it's on the Quotes and Verses handout*]: "Therefore the LORD will wait, that He may be gracious to you; and therefore He will be exalted, that He may have mercy on you. For the LORD is a God of justice; blessed are all those who wait for Him." God will wait to release His blessing until our character is ready to carry His name properly—in total integrity.

——>> **What kind of person could best carry the name of God?**

——>> **What is integrity?**

Many people want the blessings that come with God's name, but they are not ready for the temptations and challenges that will come along with such a gift.

——>> **If you walked in the total power of God, what sort of challenges might you face?**

——>> **What would people say or think about you?**

To carry God's name, we must choose to be like Jesus: humble and kind to others. Jesus was always willing to sacrifice His time, energy, and love for those around Him. He wanted them to succeed and to know all of God's love for them. We must give ourselves completely to the working of His ways within us.

——>> **The apostle Paul had a motto: "More of God and less of me!" What do you think this motto meant?**

How do we completely rid ourselves of our selfish ways? We can't, but God can. God does so by testing and refining us. Like an artist with clay, He shapes us. When you have a cut in your hand, heat draws the infection to the surface so it can be tended. In the same way God will use the heat of His testing to bring the sin in our lives to the surface. He wants us to deal with the things that hold us back from a healthy relationship with Him.

We can avoid those hard tests, but why would we want to? By ignoring them, we stop ourselves from growing in God! To have God's name placed on us, we must trust Him with the work of His testing. We must trust Him when He allows trying and despairing times to appear. If we do not turn aside, God will use that fire to help us discover all manner of evil rising from our souls. He does this so He can wipe it off and forever cast it away.

We can do ourselves a tremendous favor by giving up hiding the seriousness of our sin and becoming serious about asking God to cleanse us. Jesus died on the cross to give us the grace we need to overcome the sin in our lives. Will we run from Him, or will we trust Him? That is the test before us.

We need to ask ourselves a few questions about who we are and who we want to be. Let's all close our eyes and, in our own hearts, answer these questions as I read them.

——>> **Is there a sin in your life you've been denying the seriousness of?**

——>> **How does God view that issue?**

——>> **What will you not receive from God as long as that sin is not dealt with?**

——>> **Would you like to be free from it? Pray and ask God for forgiveness and to wipe your slate clean.**

GOD OF SACRIFICE

The cross wasn't a pretty way for the Son of God to die. Sure, Jesus' death had been predicted by a bunch of prophets. But God still could have taken it easy on his "only begotten Son." I mean, why not death by lethal injection? Jesus gets an IV, He falls asleep, they put in an overdose of morphine, and He dies quietly. It would have been so much kinder.

Why would God force Jesus to endure the most painful form of torture the ancient world knew? Nelson's Bible Dictionary doesn't mince any words in describing death by crucifixion [*Have a student read it: it's on the Quotes and Verses handout*]:

> Those sentenced to death on a cross in the Roman period were usually beaten with leather lashes—a procedure that often resulted in severe loss of blood. Victims were then generally forced to carry the upper crossbeam to the execution site, where the central stake was already set up. After being fastened to the crossbeam on the ground with ropes—or, in rare cases, nails through the wrist—the naked victim was then hoisted with the crossbeam against the standing vertical stake. A block or peg was sometimes fastened to the stake as a crude seat. The

feet were then tied or nailed to the stake. The recent discovery near Jerusalem of the bones of a crucifixion victim suggests that the knees were bent up side by side, parallel to the crossbeam, and the nail was then driven through the sides of the ankles. Death by suffocation or exhaustion normally followed only after a long period of agonizing pain.

What an awful death! Jesus understood that going to the cross was a symbol of the ultimate commitment to the Father's—and therefore His own—cause. If Jesus was willing to die for you in the most shocking and painful way imaginable, then you know He was (and remained) totally committed to you. In Matthew 10:38–39, Jesus was very specific [*Have student read Matthew 10:38–39; it's on the Quotes and Verses handout*]: "And he who does not take his cross and follow after Me is not worthy of Me. He who finds his life will lose it, and he who loses his life for My sake will find it."

Again, in Mark 10:21, Jesus asks a rich friend to follow Him wholeheartedly [*Have student read Mark 10:21; it's on the Quotes and Verses handout*]: "Then Jesus, looking at him, loved him, and said to him, 'One thing you lack: Go your way, sell whatever you have and give to the poor, and you will have treasure in heaven; and come, take up the cross, and follow Me.'" A third time, in Luke 14:27, Jesus repeatedly talks about following Him—even to the cross [*Have student read Luke 14:27; it's on the Quotes and Verses handout*]: "And whoever does not bear his cross and come after Me cannot be My disciple."

It's clear that Jesus doesn't expect us to die on a cross in order to prove our love for Him. But He does want us to be willing to do uncomfortable things in our lives if it serves God's purposes. Jesus was fully human. There's nothing He would have liked better than to have woken up on the morning of His death, summoned a bunch of angels, slaughtered His enemies, rolled over, and gone back to sleep. But He resisted that temptation, laid down His own desires, and died on that cross for all of us. The night before His arrest He wept and prayed, the Bible says, until He sweated blood. He knew what God wanted Him to do. But even He had to choose to pick up His cross and follow the will of the Father.

Paul was inspired by the way Jesus lived and the way He chose to die. Check out Philippians 2:8–11 [*Have student read Philippians 2:8–11; it's on the Quotes and Verses handout*]: "He humbled Himself and became obedient to the point of death, even the death of the cross. Therefore God also has highly exalted Him and given Him the name which is above every name, that at the name of Jesus every knee should bow, of those in heaven, and of those on earth, and of those under the earth, and that every tongue should confess that Jesus Christ is Lord. . ."

Paul spells it out even more clearly in Colossians 2:14 after talking about sin [*Have student read Colossians 2:14; it's on the Quotes and Verses handout*]: "And [Jesus] has taken it out of the way, having nailed it to the cross." Christ's sacrifice on the cross canceled the need for humans to sacrifice a goat every time they sin. The innocence of His death fulfilled God's own law and allowed Him to approach humankind again. Jesus' sacrifice enabled us to reappropriate the intimate relationship Adam had with God. "I have been crucified with Christ," Paul wrote in Galatians 2:20, "it is no longer I who live, but Christ lives in me."

Immediately after Jesus' death on the cross, cool supernatural signs happened which mirrored what was happening in the spiritual world. The earth went dark. The veil in the Temple separating the Holy of Holies—literally the place where God dwelled and where priests could only venture once a year—tore in two, allowing all believers to have access to God.

Matthew recorded in Chapter 27 that when Jesus died, "the earth quaked, and the rocks were split, and the graves were opened; and many bodies of the saints who had fallen asleep were raised; and coming out of the graves after His resurrection, they went into the holy city and appeared to many." Jesus' death awoke the spiritual dynamic of the Jewish people. Remember the Scripture about the rocks crying out if people don't worship God? Perhaps this moment was needed: with Jesus gone and His disciples scattered, it was up to the dead to spread His gospel, and the earth to shake the people out of their spiritual slumber.

So what does it all mean to us now, two thousand years and half the globe away? Nelson's Bible Dictionary boils it right down for us: "Out of the ugliness and agony of crucifixion, God accomplished the greatest good of all—the redemption of sinners."

Jesus wants us to follow in His footsteps every day, to pick up our cross and follow Him. The cross we each carry is different: we each have to make different sacrifices to serve God. Some of us have to sacrifice our thirst for money or power or good-looking girls or guys. Others have to work hard to look like Jesus and live a kind, gracious life.

But we must all do three things:

1. Ask Jesus to take control of our lives and show us the sacrifices and the blessings He expects to take from us and give to us.

2. Pick up our cross and follow Jesus by keeping His commandments every day.

3. Tell others about our experience with Jesus and how He has made us a better and happier person.

It's that simple. So, remember the sacrifice Christ made on the cross for you. And ponder whether you made the same sacrifice for Him today.

ROSARY WORKSHEET

Jesus dying on the cross is one of the most famous images in the history of humankind. It has been drawn and carved literally millions of times. Catholics, especially, are trained to remember Christ's sacrifice by observing the image of Him dying—on rosaries, in churches, and in other artwork.

The rosary is a form of prayer Catholics have used for centuries. Catholics use the beads to pray through their daily or weekly devotions. But we can use a rosary for other purposes: many Protestants use rosary beads to help them focus during prayer time.

Prayer doesn't have to be an eyes-closed, heads-bowed experience. It can be as simple as writing a note to the Lord. Let's go through this pictured rosary and scribble some of our own prayers.

[*Give out the Rosary Worksheet; remember, discussion is always good.*]

CONCLUSION

[*Pray and dismiss.*]

I AM GOD OF SACRIFICE

The rosary is a form of prayer Catholics have used for centuries. Catholics use the beads to pray through their daily or weekly devotions. But we can use a rosary for other purposes: many Protestants use rosary beads to help them focus during prayer time.

Prayer doesn't have to be an eyes-closed, heads-bowed experience. It can be as simple as writing a note to the Lord. Let's go through this pictured rosary and scribble some of our own prayers. Fill out the prayers below.

A. Adoration
God, You constantly amaze me.

You are:

1. So wise
2. So powerful
3. _____
4. _____
5. _____
6. _____
7. _____
8. _____
9. _____
10. _____

B. Thankfulness
God, I am blessed beyond what I deserve.

Thank You so much for:

1. Giving me life
2. Dying for me
3. _____
4. _____
5. _____
6. _____
7. _____
8. _____
9. _____
10. _____

C. Confession
God, I stink at so many things.

Forgive me for:

1. Judging others
2. Acting selfishly
3. _____
4. _____
5. _____
6. _____
7. _____
8. _____
9. _____
10. _____

D. Requests
Please, Lord, do Your will in my life.

Help me:

1. In school
2. Get along better with my parents
3. _____
4. _____
5. _____
6. _____
7. _____
8. _____
9. _____
10. _____

E. Unsaved friends
Lord, You're the only One who can save my friends.

Draw them closer to you:

1. _____
2. _____
3. _____
4. _____
5. _____
6. _____
7. _____
8. _____
9. _____
10. _____

I AM GOD OF SACRIFICE

1 Corinthians 10:13
"No temptation has overtaken you except such as is common to man; but God is faithful, who will not allow you to be tempted beyond what you are able, but with the temptation will also make the way of escape, that you may be able to bear it."

Isaiah 30:18
"Therefore the LORD will wait, that He may be gracious to you; and therefore He will be exalted, that He may have mercy on you. For the LORD is a God of justice; blessed are all those who wait for Him."

Nelson's Bible Dictionary
"Those sentenced to death on a cross in the Roman period were usually beaten with leather lashes—a procedure that often resulted in severe loss of blood. Victims were then generally forced to carry the upper crossbeam to the execution site, where the central stake was already set up.

After being fastened to the crossbeam on the ground with ropes—or, in rare cases, nails through the wrist—the naked victim was then hoisted with the crossbeam against the standing vertical stake. A block or peg was sometimes fastened to the stake as a crude seat. The feet were then tied or nailed to the stake. The recent discovery near Jerusalem of the bones of a crucifixion victim suggests that the knees were bent up side by side, parallel to the crossbeam, and the nail was then driven through the sides of the ankles. Death by suffocation or exhaustion normally followed only after a long period of agonizing pain."

Matthew 10:38–39
"And he who does not take his cross and follow after Me is not worthy of Me. He who finds his life will lose it, and he who loses his life for My sake will find it."

Mark 10:21
"Then Jesus, looking at him, loved him, and said to him, 'One thing you lack: Go your way, sell whatever you have and give to the poor, and you will have treasure in heaven; and come, take up the cross, and follow Me.'"

Luke 14:27
"And whoever does not bear his cross and come after Me cannot be My disciple."

Philippians 2:8–11
"He humbled Himself and became obedient to the point of death, even the death of the cross. Therefore God also has highly exalted Him and given Him the name which is above every name, that at the name of Jesus every knee should bow, of those in heaven, and of those on earth, and of those under the earth, and that every tongue should confess that Jesus Christ is Lord. . . "

Colossians 2:14
"And [Jesus] has taken it out of the way, having nailed it to the cross."

God the Reward

WHAT YOU NEED

- One copy of the curriculum for the teacher
- Bibles
- Enough copies of the Quotes and Verses handout for everyone
- Pens or pencils for each student
- Enough Reward Worksheets for everyone

RECOMMENDED READING

Teachers would greatly benefit from reading John Paul Jackson's two books *I AM: 365 Names of God* and *I AM: Inheriting the Fullness of God's Name*, both available from Streams Ministries (www.streamsministries.com or 1.888.441.8080). *I AM: 365 Names of God* is also available on a worship/meditation CD from Streams.

MULTIMEDIA IDEAS

VIDEO

If you have a video camera, drop by your favorite coffee shop and interview four or five people about what they think when they hear the word *Reward*.

INTERNET

A powerful meditation that will help you discover how your students perceive Christ can be found at http://www.embody.co.uk/archive/edb00/facetwo.swf. This Flash presentation shows a painting of Christ that can be interpreted as sad or hopeful. It might make an interesting discussion point.

Another short meditation on God's power to change our circumstances can be found at http://www.embody.co.uk/archive/eda00/dream.html.

MUSIC

"Father of Lights," the worship classic, would fit in with this presentation. The song was most recently recorded on the Vineyard Music USA release *If You Say Go*.

"River Runs," a song by the Wildings, can be found on the album *W2* from Friends Langley Vineyard. *W2* is available from Streams Ministries at www.streamsministries.com or 1.888.441.8080.

God the Reward

INTRODUCTION

God loves to give great gifts to His children. He wants to be a loving Father, giving His kids their hearts' desire. He loves to reward His servants.

——>> **What was the greatest reward you have ever received?**

——>> **What mental images do you have when someone says, "Reward"?**

——>> **What would be an appropriate reward for what you contribute to our youth group?**

Just being with God is a massive reward in itself. Abraham understood that, as we can see from Genesis 15:1 [*Have a student read Genesis 15:1; it's on the Quotes and Verses handout*]: "After these things the word of the LORD came to Abram in a vision, saying, 'Do not be afraid, Abram. I am your shield, your exceedingly great reward.'"

THE IMPORTANCE OF GOD'S NAMES

Last week we looked at the importance of sacrifice. When we pass the test God has set for us it shows Him we have become broken before Him, totally reliant on His power and grace to survive. We no longer serve our own agendas but His. And God loves that depth of sacrifice! Spiritually broken people have rejected the lie that they are okay or that they can heal themselves. Only those who walk in brokenness are clean enough to carry God's names.

Our lives are spent trying to rationalize our sin away. We give ourselves constant pep talks to try and overcome our sin: If we would just work harder or study more or practice longer or save more money or find a different church, then we could overcome our issues. These are the futile hopes of people who have yet to become broken before God. Their world is more important than God's. But to carry God's names—and the freedom that accompanies them—we must admit the hopeless reality of our human condition. We can't save ourselves, only God can.

——>> **Have you ever sinned and then tried to save yourself from the consequences of it?**

Fortunately we can give God our humanity and let Him deal with it. Spiritually broken people trade their weaknesses for the strengths of God. They live in the same hope God gave Paul in 2 Corinthians 12:9 [*Have a student read 2 Corinthians 12:9; it's on the Quotes and Verses handout*]: "My grace is sufficient for you, for My strength is made perfect in weakness."

We can trade the sin in our life for God's blessing just by asking Him for His help. This is what Jesus did on the cross for us! If we feel doubt about God or our call, we can admit it to God and trade it in for a gift of faith. If we are afraid, we can admit it to God and trade it in for His courage. Any negative emotion we feel can be given to the Lord and exchanged for His glory: anxiety traded for hope, hatred traded for love, weakness traded for strength. Our brokenness, our confession that we are weak, becomes the money needed to buy the strength and freedom God's names bring.

Individually, consider the following questions.

——>> **Is there a weakness in your life you would like to exchange for God's strength?**

——>> **How might your life be different if you were to allow this to happen?**

Relying on God is an amazing adventure. When you trust Him completely, you no longer have to work so hard to make everything happen. You can trust that He wants the best for you. Suddenly we can have the freedom simply to be God's children, and to be saved from the feeling that we must earn that right. Broken people know that God alone is their help and their reward. Even more than that, He is their very life. They live as Paul did [*Have a student read 2 Corinthians 12:10; it's on the Quotes and Verses handout*]: "Therefore I take pleasure in infirmities, in reproaches, in needs, in persecutions, in distresses, for Christ's sake. For when I am weak, then I am strong."

Our lives have to be marked not just by obedience to God but by submission to Him.

——>> Can anyone tell me the difference between obedience and submission?

The difference between obedience and submission can best be described like this. Picture a little boy, standing at the dinner table. His mom wants him to sit down. He doesn't want to. So she begs him, orders him, and threatens to punish him. Finally the little boy sits down.

As he does he looks at his mom and says, "I may be sitting down on the outside, but I'm standing up on the inside." That boy was obedient but not submissive. Even though he did what his mom said, he thought he knew better. He had to get the last word in.

Many of us act the same way with God. We sit down when He tells us to, but we grumble about it for a while. God wants His children to be submissive—to love Him so much that they trust Him when He tells them to sit down. Obeying God will only get you so far. It's actually submitting to God that unleashes many of the blessings He has for you. We must submit to God's will.

Quietly, in your heart, answer these questions.

——>> Has there been a situation in your life where you have been obedient but not submissive?

——>> What was God's plan for that situation? Did that actually occur? How do you know?

GOD THE REWARD

God does more than just replace the weakness in our life—He gives us ten times more than we could ever dream. When we look for Him, He rewards us, as we read in Hebrews 11:6 [*Have student read Hebrews 11:6; it's on the Quotes and Verses handout*]: "But without faith it is impossible to please Him, for he who comes to God must believe that He is, and that He is a rewarder of those who diligently seek Him."

God rewards us by placing His name upon each of us. He wants us to have His character in the daily routines of our lives, so we can be like Him. Sadly, many of us tell God things like "I'm so weak." We may even whine a little to God. Or we may think up any number of other excuses to avoid the submission it takes to fully carry the blessing and authority of God's name. We settle for mediocrity, for being lukewarm.

To all of us God says, "You are right where I want you, because in your weakness I will be shown strong." In the Bible anytime God wants to do something remarkable, He looks for the weakest person He can find to do it.

A perfect example of this is the life of Gideon. In Judges 6, Gideon met an angel who told him of God's plan to use him to lead the Israelites to victory. Gideon was unmoved by God's faith in him, and he answered: "God, do you have any clue who I am? Don't You know I'm from the tribe of Manasseh? Don't You know that the tribe of Manasseh is the weakest tribe in all of Israel? And not only that, my family is the weakest clan in Manasseh. Even more, I'm the weakest in all my family! So You have got to be kidding!"

I can almost hear the angel laugh as he answered, "Yes, Gideon . . . God has looked all over for you."

We need to know that God is not afraid of our weakness. He wants us to confess that we are weak so He can reward us with His love and power.

GOD THE REWARD WORKSHEET

I AM GOD THE REWARD

[*This can be done in groups, pairs, or individually.*] On your worksheets are a number of verses from the Bible that outline exactly how God interacts with us. Read each of the passages below, and then write a one-word description of the reward each one presents us. Don't just write the word; really think about what the reward might represent.

"Every good gift and every perfect gift is from above, and comes down from the Father of lights, with whom there is no variation or shadow of turning." (James 1:17)

REWARD: *A perfect gift*

"Then Amaziah said to the man of God, 'But what shall we do about the hundred talents which I have given to the troops of Israel?' And the man of God answered, 'The LORD is able to give you much more than this.'" (2 Chronicles 25:9)

REWARD: *More than just money*

"You prepare a table before me in the presence of my enemies; You anoint my head with oil; My cup runs over." (Psalm 23:5)

REWARD: *Victory over the enemy*

"A fountain of gardens, A well of living waters, And streams from Lebanon." (Song of Solomon 4:15)

REWARD: *A refreshed life full of God's living water*

"Thus says the Lord, your Redeemer, the Holy One of Israel: 'I am the LORD your God, who teaches you to profit, who leads you by the way you should go.'" (Isaiah 48:17)

REWARD: *Learning how to profit*

"In My Father's house are many mansions; if it were not so, I would have told you. I go to prepare a place for you." (John 14:2)

REWARD: *A home in Heaven*

"If any of you lacks wisdom, let him ask of God, who gives to all liberally and without reproach, and it will be given to him." (James 1:5)

REWARD: *Wisdom from God*

"The fear of the Lord is a fountain of life, to turn one away from the snares of death." (Proverbs 14:27)

REWARD: *Eternal life*

CONCLUSION

[Pray and dismiss. You may want to pray that God would reward the students as they seek Him.]

I AM GOD THE REWARD

Below are a number of verses from the Bible which outlines exactly how God interacts with us. Read each of the passages below, and then write a one-word description of the reward each one presents us. Don't just write the word; really think about what the reward might represent.

"Every good gift and every perfect gift is from above, and comes down from the Father of lights, with whom there is no variation or shadow of turning." (James 1:17)

REWARD: _____

"Then Amaziah said to the man of God, 'But what shall we do about the hundred talents which I have given to the troops of Israel?' And the man of God answered, 'The LORD is able to give you much more than this.'" (2 Chronicles 25:9)

REWARD: _____

"You prepare a table before me in the presence of my enemies; You anoint my head with oil; My cup runs over." (Psalm 23:5)

REWARD: _____

"A fountain of gardens, a well of living waters, and streams from Lebanon." (Song of Solomon 4:15)

REWARD: _____

"Thus says the Lord, your Redeemer, the Holy One of Israel: 'I am the LORD your God, who teaches you to profit, who leads you by the way you should go.'" (Isaiah 48:17)

REWARD: _____

"In My Father's house are many mansions; if it were not so, I would have told you. I go to prepare a place for you." (John 14:2)

REWARD: _____

"If any of you lacks wisdom, let him ask of God, who gives to all liberally and without reproach, and it will be given to him." (James 1:5)

REWARD: _____

"The fear of the Lord is a fountain of life, to turn one away from the snares of death." (Proverbs 14:27)

REWARD: _____

I AM GOD THE REWARD

Genesis 15:1
"After these things the word of the LORD came to Abram in a vision, saying, 'Do not be afraid, Abram. I am your shield, your exceedingly great reward.'"

2 Corinthians 12:9
"My grace is sufficient for you, for My strength is made perfect in weakness."

2 Corinthians 12:10
"Therefore I take pleasure in infirmities, in reproaches, in needs, in persecutions, in distresses, for Christ's sake. For when I am weak, then I am strong."

Hebrews 11:6
"But without faith it is impossible to please Him, for he who comes to God must believe that He is, and that He is a rewarder of those who diligently seek Him."

WHAT YOU NEED

- One copy of the curriculum for the teacher

- This session is vastly different from the others and will require some advance planning by your team. To better understand God's merciful nature, we suggest taking the opportunity to perform acts of kindness. A list of suggestions is attached, but you know your students and community better than anyone else: plan an initiative that is needed and will appeal to your group. Be as creative as possible!

- There is a brief introduction to I AM God of Mercy attached.

RECOMMENDED READING

Teachers would greatly benefit from reading John Paul Jackson's two books *I AM: 365 Names of God* and *I AM: Inheriting the Fullness of God's Name*, both available from Streams Ministries (www.streamsministries.com or 1.888.441.8080). *I AM: 365 Names of God* is also available on a worship/meditation CD from Streams.

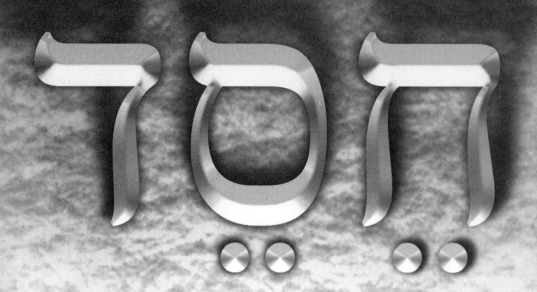

God of Mercy

INTRODUCTION

God's mercy is one of the most powerful themes running through the Bible. It's incredible when you think about it: a perfect God showing mercy to His creation in countless different ways. When the Israelites were starving in the desert, He made bread fall like rain every morning to feed them. When David committed adultery and murder, God—in His mercy—forgave him.

Today we will spread the mercy of God to others by performing a few simple activities.

GOD OF MERCY

Very quickly let's look at why we should show mercy to others.

——>> Can anyone here tell me what mercy is?

Mercy is not getting what you deserve; rather, it's getting what you DON'T deserve. God loves to show us His kindness, especially when we don't deserve it. That's why He loves forgiving our sin: He knows we don't deserve His mercy, but He loves to give it to us anyway. Exodus 22:27 tells us that God is gracious. Isaiah 43:25 says that God will not remember our sins. These are foundational truths about the nature and mercy of God that we can believe in.

What an amazing gift God's mercy is! Our job on earth is to reflect the mercy He has shown us by being merciful to others. "We love because He first loved us," the apostle John wrote. Today is our chance to show others what God has given us: love. So let's do it!

OUTFLOW

[Explain the merciful acts you are going to be doing today. And do them!]

I AM GOD OF MERCY

IDEAS FOR MERCY OUTFLOW

You know your community and your students better than anyone; try to plan some creative activities that will appeal to them and benefit the community. Below are a few suggestions done in other churches:

- Clean up and beautify your church grounds, a local school or park, or a senior center. This could include picking up trash, planting flowers, gardening, painting, or other projects. Get permission first! One youth group we know spent a summer day cleaning up a park and fountain. After filling ten bags of garbage, they had a fountain party—complete with a barbecue, air mattresses, and Beach Boys' music. They even ended up with their picture on the front page of the local newspaper.

- Start a drive of some sort. A food drive, clothing drive, coin drive, book drive. Find a need, and look to fill it. One church we know puts together Christmas hampers for families. Every small group and ministry in the church adopts one family and puts together age-and gender-specific gifts for the kids and fun stuff for the parents.

- Visit a home for the aged. One youth group we know actually went to a long-term-care facility on Halloween and carved pumpkins with the seniors. The old folks loved it, and the kids had a great time!

- Prepare a special meal or dessert. Bless some people with a delicious meal. One church we know made soup every Sunday for its attendees. This helped forge community—and fill stomachs!

- Teach someone else's Sunday School. Give the regular teachers a surprise break by teaching Sunday School one morning. Have a blast with the kids.

- Wash cars in the church parking lot. Create a designated "car wash" section of the parking lot where people can park and get their cars washed. Refuse to take any donations!

- On a rainy day get as many umbrellas as possible, and help people get to and from their cars without getting wet. This can be done at church, at the shopping center, or at a grocery store.

- Have a Custodian Appreciation Day. Clean the church top to bottom. Make a card telling your cleaning staff how much they're appreciated. Leave them some money for coffee.

- Free coffee or hot chocolate station. Set up a spot at church or in the community where you give away free hot chocolate and coffee.

- Go Christmas caroling. A youth group we know has gone caroling for several years at a local hospital. They bring their guitars and go from room to room in the extended care wing. Be prepared to pray with people!

God of Every Creature

WHAT YOU NEED

- One copy of the curriculum for the teacher
- Bibles
- Enough copies of the Quotes and Verses handout for everyone
- Pens or pencils for each student
- Copies of the Skit for each actor

RECOMMENDED READING

Teachers would greatly benefit from reading John Paul Jackson's two books *I AM: 365 Names of God* and *I AM: Inheriting the Fullness of God's Name*, both available from Streams Ministries (www.streamsministries.com or 1.888.441.8080). *I AM: 365 Names of God* is also available on a worship/meditation CD from Streams.

MULTIMEDIA IDEAS

POWERPOINT
We suggest illustrating the story of Balaam and his donkey with slides from a website that has put some biblical stories into Lego form. You can go directly to Balaam's story at http://www.thereverend.com/brick_testament/the_wilderness/balaams_talking_donkey/nm22_21.html. We should warn you, however: some of the site is very disrespectful and not suitable for all ages. This link, however, will take you straight to the story of Balaam and is fine.

MUSIC
"Let Everything that Has Breath," featured on Matt Redman's *The Heart of Worship* album—and countless others, would fit in well with this session.

"I'll Give You All of My Life," a Flood cut from the Langley Vineyard release *The Well: Live in the Spirit*, would also fit in with this session. *The Well* can be ordered from Streams Ministries at 1.888.441.8080 or at www.streamsministries.com.

You can find "Wonderful Maker" on Matt Redman's album *Where Angels Fear to Tread*, available from Streams Ministries at 1.888.441.8080 or at www.streamsministries.com.

God of Every Creature

INTRODUCTION

Everything everywhere was created by God. Think of the magnitude of that for a moment. Every particle, every atom, every thing, every person, was created by God. From fish to angels, He made it. From grass to mountains, He formed it.

—>> **What's the strangest thing God has made?**

—>> **Why did He create it?**

Because of this fact, God calls Himself the God of Every Creature. Everything on earth is His.

THE IMPORTANCE OF GOD'S NAMES

Last week we tried to show God's mercy to others by performing an act of kindness. God's great mercy toward us is based upon His name. He wants to bond with us and make us one with Him, according to 1 Corinthians 6:17 [*Have student read 1 Corinthians 6:17; it's on the Quotes and Verses handout*]: "He who is joined to the Lord is one spirit with Him."

Becoming one with the Lord is just the beginning. Those who are one in Spirit with the Lord are called to take on His attributes, and this means taking on His name. This goes far beyond just calling ourselves "Christian." In fact, God's very name is at stake in you!

When God saved us, He said, "Welcome. You are called by My name, and I am going to put that name on you. It doesn't matter what you think about yourself—I know where you're going, and I know why I created you. I love you more than anything else. I am not only going to put My name on you, but I'm going to prepare you to bear it. Why? Because I will not put anything on you that is greater than what you can bear. You will feel like you can't handle it, but you will, because I will prepare you and enable you to carry it. You will carry My name to the world."

As we learn to embrace God's work in our lives, we will soon begin to reap the blessings of bearing His name. No matter what the cost we pay in the work of preparation, it will never compare with the blessings we gain from being marked by His name.

Of all the blessings found in bearing God's name, one stands above the rest: salvation. This is the very core of what Jesus Christ has done for those who carry His name. As Acts 4:12 says [*Have a student read Acts 4:12; it's on the Quotes and Verses handout*]: "Salvation is found in no one else, for there is no other name under heaven given to men by which we must be saved."

Without Jesus we were lost and without hope. Still, out of His tremendous love, He has given us His name and the hope that comes with it. Salvation is not merely the eternal life we enter into when we die; rather, it is a quality of life we can experience right now—a life filled with His presence. David sang about this life in Psalm 16:11 [*Have a student read Psalm 16:11; it's on the Quotes and Verses handout*]: "You will show me the path of life; in Your presence is fullness of joy; at Your right hand are pleasures forevermore."

> ——>> **Have you ever experienced God's joy? Do you know someone who has?**

> ——>> **What was that experience like?**

> ——>> **When you look at your life before and after meeting Christ, how has it changed?**

The presence of the Lord releases His saving power—power to destroy hopelessness, power to bring healing, power to defeat fear, and power to overcome the sin in our lives. This is what it means to walk in the saving power of God, and this is the blessing that awaits those who bear His name.

As we learn how to bear God's name, we become respected and honored among people, and this causes God's name to grow in renown. God becomes famous through what He does with us. As He allows us to experience His mighty acts and give Him the honor for it, our lives give

Him glory. And people notice!

When we learn to cling to the Lord, we become vehicles that bring Him great honor. Clinging to Him takes passion and loyalty. Those who cling to the Lord are those who love to worship Him. Isaiah understood this principle: he declared that we were all created to give God praise (Isaiah 43:21). In Romans 9:17 we again see that God created us for the purpose of bringing glory to His name [*Have a student read Romans 9:17; it's on the Quotes and Verses handout*]: "For the Scripture says to the Pharaoh, 'For this very purpose I have raised you up, that I may show My power in you, and that My name may be declared in all the earth.'"

God wants to pour His glory through us, as long as our hearts are humble and faithful. If we are humble, God will entrust us with everything. He hungers for this so that His greatness will be displayed to the world and so that more people will be freed from serving the empire of evil.

I AM GOD OF EVERY CREATURE

Just as we reflect God's nature to those who don't know Him, so does the rest of His creation. Everything He has made reflects Him in some way—and can teach us about who He is.

For example, an oyster sits at the bottom of the ocean, forming its own shell of protection from aragonite mineral sheets and conchiolin protein. Inside, it is soft and safe from oyster-eaters. Sometimes, however, something gets inside that shell: a small bit of food, for example. The oyster's soft inside is irritated by the particle and begins to fight it with its shell-building mineral and protein. Eventually, that little bit of food is turned into a pearl.

> ——>> **What can we learn about God by studying how an oyster forms a pearl?**

[*Guide the discussion wherever it goes, but most classes will come up with an answer like "God turns the common into something priceless."*]

Sometimes the way God speaks to us through His creation isn't even that obscure. The Bible records one time when a donkey told his rider exactly what to do. In fact, I have a skit we can perform to illustrate this story: I just need three volunteers. [*Pick three people, give them the skit, and have them perform it.*]

THE GOD OF EVERY CREATURE SKIT

CHARACTERS
Balaam
Donkey
Angel
The Narrator (should be the group facilitator)

SETTING
Balaam is "riding" his donkey. The Angel is hidden somewhere.

SKIT

Narrator *(loudly, as an introduction to the group)*: One day a man named Balaam went to talk with a mighty king. He wasn't sure if he should go, but in the end he saddled up his trusty donkey and off they went.

Balaam: Faster, Donkey!

Narrator: Suddenly an Angel of the Lord appeared and stood in the Donkey's way. Naturally Balaam couldn't see the Angel—but the donkey did!

Donkey bucks Balaam off her back.

Balaam *(climbs back on the Donkey)*: Stupid Donkey! What's the matter with you!

Balaam tries to get the Donkey to move, but she won't budge. Balaam slaps the Donkey, pushes the Donkey, pulls the Donkey, drags the Donkey. But the Donkey won't move.

Donkey *(madly)*: What have I done to make you strike me like this?

Balaam: You refuse to move! You're lucky I don't have a sword in my hand—or you'd be dead!

Donkey: Have I ever done this before? Haven't you had me for many years?

Balaam: No, you've never acted like this before.

Angel: Perhaps I can explain…

Balaam *(shocked)*: What?!? Where did you come from?

Angel: Why did you hit your donkey? You're lucky she was paying attention—if you had run into me, I would have killed you and spared her!

Donkey: Thank you very much.

Angel: No problem at all. Is Balaam always such a jerk?

Donkey: Yes. Yes, he is.

Balaam *(sadly)*: O Angel, I have sinned! You stood in the way to stop me, and I kept pushing on. I'm sorry.

Narrator: Eventually, the Angel gave Balaam permission to meet with the evil king, but first he had to promise to speak only the words God gave him.

(Thunderous applause.)

GOD OF EVERY CREATURE

When humans fail to understand the depth of God's power and love, the Bible teaches us that creation steps up to announce that truth. Jesus Himself said in Luke 19:40 [*Have a student read Luke 19:40; it's on the Quotes and Verses handout*]: "I tell you if these should keep silent, the stones would immediately cry out."

——>> **What do you think a rock would say about God?**

——>> **Do you think Jesus meant this literally or figuratively? That is, did He really mean rocks themselves would cry out, or did He mean that creation generally speaks about God anyway?**

There are many examples of people who have been touched by the beauty of God's creation. One such man's name was John Muir. In 1867 Muir was fixing a machine in an Indianapolis factory. His hand slipped, and a spike fell through his fingers and punctured his eyes. Muir was completely blinded.

Desperate and lying in a hospital bed, Muir prayed that God would heal him, promising to dedicate the rest of his life to exploring the most precious sights that had been taken away from him—God's marvelous creation.

Over several months his sight miraculously returned, and Muir, true to his word, traveled throughout North America for the rest of his life. He walked from Kentucky to Florida to California to Alaska, but it was a large patch of land called Yosemite that captivated him [*Have a student read Muir's thoughts on Yosemite; it's on the Quotes and Verses handout*]: "Full of God's thoughts, a place of peace and safety amid the most exalted grandeur and eager enthusiastic action, a new song . . . with sermons in stones, storms, trees, flowers, and animals brimful with humanity."

——>> **Have you ever felt God somewhere in His creation?**

Muir formed an environmental group called the Sierra Club in 1892 to help him convince the government to set aside Yosemite as a national park. The club was successful, and to this day Americans enjoy the park Muir built. In fact, Muir is called the grandfather of environmentalism. Not bad for a Christian man who was blind in his early twenties! Muir's healing changed the continent, and more than a century later his wonderment at God's creation still inspires men and women to seek God [*Have a student read Muir's comment on God's first temples: it's on the Quotes and Verses handout*]: "Every hidden cell is throbbing with music and life, every fiber thrilling like harp strings, while incense is ever flowing from the balsam bells and leaves. No wonder the hills and groves were God's first temples."

Muir changed the world because of his love for God's creation. Balaam was almost killed by an angel because of the way he abused his donkey. God wants us to look for the pieces of His nature He has placed in every one of His creations.

If we truly love God, we must never forget the words of 1 Chronicles 29:11 [*Have a student read 1 Chronicles 29:11; it's on the Quotes and Verses handout*]: "Yours, O LORD, is the greatness, the power and the glory, the victory and the majesty; for all that is in heaven and in earth is Yours; Yours is the kingdom, O LORD, and You are exalted as head over all."

CONCLUSION

[*Pray and dismiss. Ask God to be the Lord of each student, and to have Him reveal Himself to the class through His creation this week.*]

I AM GOD OF EVERY CREATURE

CHARACTERS
Balaam
Donkey
Angel
The Narrator (*should be the group facilitator*)

SETTING
Balaam is "riding" his donkey. The Angel is hidden somewhere.

SKIT

Narrator (*loudly, as an introduction to the group*): One day a man named Balaam went to talk with a mighty king. He wasn't sure if he should go, but in the end he saddled up his trusty donkey and off they went.

Balaam: Faster, Donkey!

Narrator: Suddenly an Angel of the Lord appeared and stood in the Donkey's way. Naturally Balaam couldn't see the Angel—but the donkey did!

Donkey bucks Balaam off her back.

Balaam (*climbs back on the Donkey*): Stupid Donkey! What's the matter with you!

Balaam tries to get the Donkey to move, but she won't budge. Balaam slaps the Donkey, pushes the Donkey, pulls the Donkey, drags the Donkey. But the Donkey won't move.

Donkey (*madly*): What have I done to make you strike me like this?

Balaam: You refuse to move! You're lucky I don't have a sword in my hand—or you'd be dead!

Donkey: Have I ever done this before? Haven't you had me for many years?

Balaam: No, you've never acted like this before.

Angel: Perhaps I can explain…

Balaam (*shocked*): What?!? Where did you come from?

Angel: Why did you hit your donkey? You're lucky she was paying attention—if you had run into me, I would have killed you and spared her!

Donkey: Thank you very much.

Angel: No problem at all. Is Balaam always such a jerk?

Donkey: Yes. Yes, he is.

Balaam (*sadly*)**:** O Angel, I have sinned! You stood in the way to stop me, and I kept pushing on. I'm sorry.

Narrator: Eventually the Angel gave Balaam permission to meet with the evil king, but first he had to promise to speak only the words God gave him.

(*Thunderous applause.*)

I AM GOD OF EVERY CREATURE

1 Corinthians 6:17
"He who is joined to the Lord is one spirit with Him."

Acts 4:12, NIV
"Salvation is found in no one else, for there is no other name under heaven given to men by which we must be saved."

Psalm 16:11
"You will show me the path of life; in Your presence is fullness of joy; at Your right hand are pleasures forevermore."

Romans 9:17
"For the Scripture says to the Pharaoh, 'For this very purpose I have raised you up, that I may show My power in you, and that My name may be declared in the earth.'"

Luke 19:40
"I tell you that if these should keep silent, the stones would immediately cry out."

John Muir on Yosemite
"Full of God's thoughts, a place of peace and safety amid the most exalted grandeur and eager enthusiastic action, a new song . . . with sermons in stones, storms, trees, flowers, and animals brimful with humanity."

John Muir on God's First Temples
"Every hidden cell is throbbing with music and life, every fiber thrilling like harp strings, while incense is ever flowing from the balsam bells and leaves. No wonder the hills and groves were God's first temples."

1 Chronicles 29:11
"Yours, O LORD, is the greatness, The power and the glory, The victory and the majesty; For all that is in heaven and in earth is Yours; Yours is the kingdom, O LORD, And You are exalted as head over all."

God the Ancient One

WHAT YOU NEED

- One copy of the curriculum for the teacher
- Bibles
- One copy of the Quotes and Verses handout for each student
- Pens or pencils for each student
- Three copies of the skit
- One set of the three worksheets for each student (they'll do them in groups)

RECOMMENDED READING

 Teachers would greatly benefit from reading John Paul Jackson's two books *I AM: 365 Names of God* and *I AM: Inheriting the Fullness of God's Name*, both available from Streams Ministries (www.streamsministries.com or 1.888.441.8080). *I AM: 365 Names of God* is also available on a worship/meditation CD from Streams.

MULTIMEDIA IDEAS

 ### POWERPOINT
A slide show of ancient structures and ruins might be a cool effect to use. Visit http://www.freefoto.com, and do a search for *ancient* or *ruins*, and see the pictures that come up. Another great site is http://www.undiscoveredscotland.co.uk/uswallpaper/index.html.

 ### COMPUTER ANIMATION
A California-based ministry called Highway Video produces high-quality, trendy animations for church groups. If you log on to www.highwayvideo.com and purchase their VIBE Videos, Vol. 4, you will receive five great presentations that can be used throughout this twelve-week course. For this week's class we suggest showing "Candlelight," which features a video of several different candles burning.

 ### INTERNET
Anno Domini, a presentation of the Virtual Museum of Canada, records artwork done of Jesus through the ages. It can be found online at http://www.virtualmuseum.ca/Exhibitions/Annodomini/entrance-en.html.

VIDEO
The skit in this session is a reenactment of the burning bush scene in the animated film *The Prince of Egypt*. You could show it in conjunction with, or instead of, doing the skit.

Watch the local listings for your local history or learning network, and tape a show that includes pictures of archaeological discoveries or ruins. This would be handy to have playing in the background during your session.

 ### SONGS
"Long to Know You" and "Sunrise," two great songs by Chris Janzen, can be found on the album *W2* from Friends Langley Vineyard, available from Streams Ministries (www.streamsministries.com or 1.888.441.8080). Both songs speak to the timelessness of one's relationship with God.

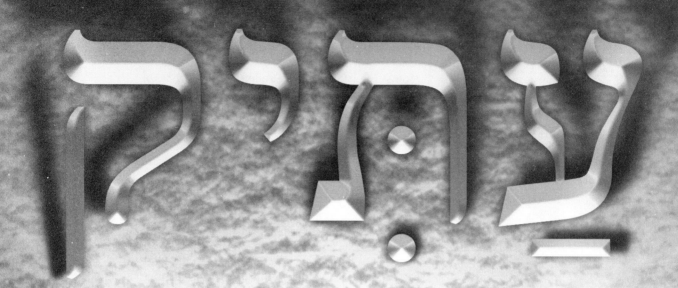

God the Ancient One

INTRODUCTION

It's hard for our human brains to imagine, but before the world existed, God was there, as we can read in Genesis 1:2 [*Have a student read Genesis 1:2; it's on the Quotes and Verses handout*]: "The earth was without form, and void; and darkness was on the face of the deep. And the Spirit of God was hovering over the face of the waters." He created everything we know that exists. After forming the earth and the heavens, God created humankind and began to forge a relationship with us. Adam, Eve, Abel, Enoch, Noah, Abraham, Sarah, Isaac, Jacob, Joseph, Moses, Deborah, Gideon, Samson, Samuel, David, Solomon: they all lived out the history of how God has interacted with men and women. Thanks to His ancient ways, we are able to know how He wants to interact with us.

Being a Christian makes us part of a long history of amazing people. We are able to live under the promises and blessings God gave our ancestors.

—>> **What can we learn about God from knowing how He has dealt with humans throughout history?**

—>> **What can we learn from how God deals with us today?**

THE IMPORTANCE OF GOD'S NAMES

Let's continue our look at the importance of the names of God. In Old Testament times priests had the words *Holy unto the Lord* written on their foreheads. Likewise, we need to carry the names of God in our life. Doing so makes us safe in His care, as David mentioned in Psalm 20:7, NASB [*Have a student read Psalm 20:7; it's on the Quotes and Verses handout*]: "Some boast in chariots, and some in horses; but we will boast in the name of the Lord, our God." To carry God's name properly, we must understand what it will cost. We must realize what such a life will look like.

God is calling us to be a people marked by His name, to be willing to have all ungodliness and impurity removed from our hearts. As Christians, we will be stretched and have to deal with new issues He will reveal to us as we grow in Him. While our friends are getting away with certain behavior, God will call us to a higher standard of purity. All of those old, lesser things will need to fall by the wayside, because His name needs to become more important to us than anything else. In order for God to create the necessary purity in our lives, He will have to help us in submitting different areas of our lives to Him. One of those areas is our affections. God wants to align our heart perfectly with His. He wants us to lose any affection that might steal the focus of our heart away from Him. The Bible speaks of the Church as the bride of Christ. Traditionally, every bride is given the name of her husband. So, too, we have been given the name of Jesus. To put it more clearly, God wants us to love the things He loves.

> **——>> Do you understand what we mean by affections?**

> **——>> What do you think God wants you to love?**

Another thing God wants us to give to Him is our thoughts. A life that is marked by the name of the Lord is a life that is pure at the level of thinking. We can learn to focus our thoughts on whatever is pure, right, holy, and good—as we're told to do in Philippians 4:8—rather than on any of the cares and concerns of this world—which is always where the world pushes us to focus.

> **——>> What do you think God thinks about?**

Another part of us that God wants to use is our actions. Those who are marked by the name of the Lord are freed from things that can distract them from fully pursuing Him. We need to ask ourselves questions like "Why am I doing this?" God is calling us to be mindful of the activities we give ourselves to—we can no longer afford to waste our energy on things that don't really matter and are not truly good for us.

> **——>> What do you do right now that you think God loves to see?**

Another thing God wants us to look at is our time. How do we use our time? Do we waste it on ourselves, or do we spend it on others by serving them? A life that is marked by the name of the Lord does not hang on to time as though it were its own.

> **——>> Where do you waste the most time?**

> **——>> How much time do you spend helping others?**

——>> **Do you think God wants you to spend time doing things you love?**

The final part of our life God wants to influence is our money. Money is a tough one: everyone likes to have lots of it. But a life that is marked by the name of the Lord does not hold on to money as a security blanket. Instead, Christians need to be the most generous people on earth. The early Church understood this idea [*Have a student read Acts 20:35; it's on the Quotes and Verses handout*]: "It is more blessed to give than to receive."

——>> **Does anyone here have a job?**

——>> **How do you spend your money?**

——>> **How much money have you given away lately?**

God is not just looking for people who are obedient; rather, He is seeking people who are submissive to His will. God is looking for willing vessels He can trust and upon whom He can put His name. This is His dream for you.

I AM GOD THE ANCIENT ONE

The best place to learn about God is in the Bible. In Scripture we can see how God interacts with men and women just like us. We can then better understand His nature.

Let's look at a few examples of how God interacted with ancient figures. Moses is one of the most famous people in the Bible, thanks to movies like *The Prince of Egypt*. Moses was just a shepherd, trying to raise a family in the desert, when God revealed Himself to him. *The Prince of Egypt* recorded Moses' encounter at the Burning Bush . . . and we have a skit reenacting that pivotal moment in Moses' life. I'll need two volunteers [*set up for and do the Skit*].

SESSION 11—THE SKIT
(I AM GOD THE ANCIENT ONE)

CHARACTERS
Moses
The Burning Bush
The Narrator (*should be the group facilitator*)

SETTING
Moses is looking at a burning bush.

SKIT

Narrator (*loudly, as an introduction to the group*): Moses had been banished from Egypt for his crimes and had lived in the desert for almost twenty years when, one day, God met him and changed everything. On that fateful day Moses saw a burning bush, which, while obviously on fire, was not being consumed by that flame.

Burning Bush: Moses.

Moses *(hesitantly)*: Here I am!

Burning Bush: Take the sandals from your feet. The place on which you stand is holy ground.

Moses takes his shoes off.

Moses: Who are you?

Burning Bush: I AM WHO I AM.

Moses *(confused)*: I don't understand.

Burning Bush: I am the God of your ancestors, Abraham, Isaac, and Jacob.

Moses: What do you want with me?

Burning Bush: I have seen the oppression of my people in Egypt. And have heard their cries. So I have come down to deliver them out of slavery. And bring them to a good land. A land flowing with milk and honey. And so to Pharaoh I shall send you.

Moses *(scared)*: Me? Who am I to lead these people? They'll never believe me—they won't even listen.

Burning Bush: I shall teach you what to say.

Moses: But I was their enemy. I was the Prince of Egypt. The son of the man who slaughtered their children. You've chosen the wrong messenger. How can I even speak to these people?

Burning Bush: WHO MADE MAN'S MOUTH? WHO MADE THE DEAF, THE SEEING, OR THE BLIND? DID NOT I? NOW GO!!!!!!

Moses flinches, scared of God's awesome power.

Burning Bush *(gently)*: Go, Moses. I shall go with you when you go to the king of Egypt. But Pharaoh will not listen. So I will stretch out my hand. And smite Egypt with all my wonders! Take the staff in your hand. With it you shall do my wonders! I shall be with you, Moses.

(Thunderous applause.)

WORKSHEETS AND CONCLUSION

Did you notice how God introduced Himself to Moses? He said, "I am the God of your ancestors, Abraham, Isaac, and Jacob." He did this to direct Moses to learn more about the great promise and relationship that had existed between God and those three men. God wasn't starting at square one with Moses, revealing Himself for the first time. Moses could, if he wanted to, find out more about how the Lord had interacted with his forebearers.

But what would Moses have learned about God from the lives of Abraham, Isaac, and Jacob?

144

The same things we can learn.

[Divide the class into small groups, and give them the worksheets included. Have them discuss the questions. If time permits, have a group discussion about their findings. When they're finished, pray and dismiss.]

SESSION 11—SMALL GROUP: 1 (ABRAHAM)
I AM GOD THE ANCIENT ONE

A. Read the following verses.

Genesis 15:1
"After these things the word of the LORD came to Abram in a vision, saying, 'Do not be afraid, Abram. I am your shield, your exceedingly great reward.'"

Genesis 15:12–16
"Now when the sun was going down, a deep sleep fell upon Abram; and behold, horror and great darkness fell upon him. Then He said to Abram: 'Know certainly that your descendants will be strangers in a land that is not theirs, and will serve them, and they will afflict them four hundred years. And also the nation whom they serve I will judge; afterward they shall come out with great possessions. Now as for you, you shall go to your fathers in peace; you shall be buried at a good old age. But in the fourth generation they shall return here, for the iniquity of the Amorites is not yet complete.'"

Genesis 17:1–6
"When Abram was ninety-nine years old, the LORD appeared to Abram and said to him, 'I am Almighty God; walk before Me and be blameless. And I will make My covenant between Me and you, and will multiply you exceedingly.' Then Abram fell on his face, and God talked with him, saying: 'As for Me, behold, My covenant is with you, and you shall be a father of many nations. No longer shall your name be called Abram, but your name shall be Abraham; for I have made you a father of many nations. I will make you exceedingly fruitful; and I will make nations of you, and kings shall come from you.'"

B. Discuss and answer the following questions.

1. What does it mean to have God as your shield and reward?

2. What was God promising Abraham?

3. What would this story tell Moses about the Israelites' life in Egypt?

4. What can we glean about God's nature in this story for our present-day lives as Christians?

I AM GOD THE ANCIENT ONE

A. Read the following verses.

Genesis 26:1–5
"There was a famine in the land, besides the first famine that was in the days of Abraham. And Isaac went to Abimelech king of the Philistines, in Gerar. Then the LORD appeared to him and said: 'Do not go down to Egypt; live in the land of which I shall tell you. Dwell in this land, and I will be with you and bless you; for to you and your descendants I give all these lands, and I will perform the oath which I swore to Abraham your father. And I will make your descendants multiply as the stars of heaven; I will give to your descendants all these lands; and in your seed all the nations of the earth shall be blessed; because Abraham obeyed My voice and kept My charge, My commandments, My statutes, and My laws.'"

Genesis 26:24
"And the LORD appeared to him the same night and said, 'I am the God of your father Abraham; do not fear, for I am with you. I will bless you and multiply your descendants for My servant Abraham's sake.'"

B. Discuss and answer the following questions.

1. Why did God take such good care of Isaac?

2. What was God promising Isaac?

3. What would this story tell Moses about the nature of God?

4. What can we glean about God's nature in this story for our present-day lives as Christians?

5. How can we learn and keep God's charge, statutes, commandments, and laws?

I AM GOD THE ANCIENT ONE

A. Read the following verses.

Genesis 28:10–22
"Now Jacob went out from Beersheba and went toward Haran. So he came to a certain place and stayed there all night, because the sun had set. And he took one of the stones of that place and put it at his head, and he lay down in that place to sleep. Then he dreamed, and behold, a ladder was set up on the earth, and its top reached to heaven; and there the angels of God were ascending and descending on it.

And behold, the LORD stood above it and said: 'I am the LORD God of Abraham your father and the God of Isaac; the land on which you lie I will give to you and your descendants. Also your descendants shall be as the dust of the earth; you shall spread abroad to the west and the east, to the north and the south; and in you and in your seed all the families of the earth shall be blessed. Behold, I am with you and will keep you wherever you go, and will bring you back to this land; for I will not leave you until I have done what I have spoken to you.'

Then Jacob awoke from his sleep and said, 'Surely the LORD is in this place, and I did not know it.' And he was afraid and said, 'How awesome is this place! This is none other than the house of God, and this is the gate of heaven!' Then Jacob rose early in the morning, and took the stone that he had put at his head, set it up as a pillar, and poured oil on top of it. And he called the name of that place Bethel; but the name of that city had been Luz previously. Then Jacob made a vow, saying, 'If God will be with me, and keep me in this way that I am going, and give me bread to eat and clothing to put on, so that I come back to my father's house in peace, then the LORD shall be my God. And this stone which I have set as a pillar shall be God's house, and of all that You give me I will surely give a tenth to You.'"

B. Discuss and answer the following questions.

1. What does Jacob's response to God teach us about obedience?

2. What was God promising Jacob?

3. What would this story tell Moses about the Israelites' life in Egypt?

4. What can we glean about God's nature in this story for our present-day lives as Christians?

I AM GOD THE ANCIENT ONE

CHARACTERS
Moses
The Burning Bush
The Narrator (should be the group facilitator)

SETTING
Moses is looking at a burning bush.

SKIT

Narrator *(loudly, as an introduction to the group)*: Moses had been banished from Egypt for his crimes and had lived in the desert for almost twenty years when, one day, God met him and changed everything. On that fateful day Moses saw a burning bush, which, while obviously on fire, was not being consumed by that flame.

Burning Bush: Moses.

Moses *(hesitantly)*: Here I am!

Burning Bush: Take the sandals from your feet. The place on which you stand is holy ground.

Moses takes his shoes off.

Moses: Who are you?

Burning Bush: I AM WHO I AM.

Moses *(confused)*: I don't understand.

Burning Bush: I am the God of your ancestors, Abraham, Isaac, and Jacob.

Moses: What do you want with me?

Burning Bush: I have seen the oppression of my people in Egypt. And have heard their cries. So I have come down to deliver them out of slavery. And bring them to a good land. A land flowing with milk and honey. And so to Pharaoh I shall send you.

Moses *(scared)*: Me? Who am I to lead these people? They'll never believe me—they won't even listen.

Burning Bush: I shall teach you what to say.

Moses: But I was their enemy. I was the Prince of Egypt. The son of the man who slaughtered their children. You've chosen the wrong messenger. How can I even speak to these people?

Burning Bush: WHO MADE MAN'S MOUTH? WHO MADE THE DEAF, THE SEEING, OR THE BLIND? DID NOT I? NOW GO!!!!!!

Moses flinches, scared of God's awesome power.

Burning Bush (*gently*): Go, Moses. I shall go with you when you go to the king of Egypt. But Pharaoh will not listen. So I will stretch out my hand. And smite Egypt with all my wonders! Take the staff in your hand. With it you shall do my wonders! I shall be with you, Moses.

(*Thunderous applause.*)

I AM GOD THE ANCIENT ONE

A. Read the following verses.

Genesis 15:1
"After these things the word of the LORD came to Abram in a vision, saying, 'Do not be afraid, Abram. I am your shield, your exceedingly great reward.'"

Genesis 15:12–16
"Now when the sun was going down, a deep sleep fell upon Abram; and behold, horror and great darkness fell upon him. Then He said to Abram: 'Know certainly that your descendants will be strangers in a land that is not theirs, and will serve them, and they will afflict them four hundred years. And also the nation whom they serve I will judge; afterward they shall come out with great possessions. Now as for you, you shall go to your fathers in peace; you shall be buried at a good old age. But in the fourth generation they shall return here, for the iniquity of the Amorites is not yet complete.'"

Genesis 17:1–6
"When Abram was ninety-nine years old, the LORD appeared to Abram and said to him, 'I am Almighty God; walk before Me and be blameless. And I will make My covenant between Me and you, and will multiply you exceedingly.' Then Abram fell on his face, and God talked with him, saying: 'As for Me, behold, My covenant is with you, and you shall be a father of many nations. No longer shall your name be called Abram, but your name shall be Abraham; for I have made you a father of many nations. I will make you exceedingly fruitful; and I will make nations of you, and kings shall come from you.'"

B. Discuss and answer the following questions.

1. What does it mean to have God as your shield and reward?

2. What was God promising Abraham?

3. What would this story tell Moses about the Israelites' life in Egypt?

4. What can we glean about God's nature in this story for present-day lives as Christians?

I AM GOD THE ANCIENT ONE

A. Read the following verses.

Genesis 26:1–5
"There was a famine in the land, besides the first famine that was in the days of Abraham. And Isaac went to Abimelech king of the Philistines, in Gerar. Then the LORD appeared to him and said: 'Do not go down to Egypt; live in the land of which I shall tell you. Dwell in this land, and I will be with you and bless you; for to you and your descendants I give all these lands, and I will perform the oath which I swore to Abraham your father. And I will make your descendants multiply as the stars of heaven; I will give to your descendants all these lands; and in your seed all the nations of the earth shall be blessed; because Abraham obeyed My voice and kept My charge, My commandments, My statutes, and My laws.'"

Genesis 26:24
"And the LORD appeared to him the same night and said, 'I am the God of your father Abraham; do not fear, for I am with you. I will bless you and multiply your descendants for My servant Abraham's sake.'"

B. Discuss and answer the following questions.

1. Why did God take such good care of Isaac?

2. What was God promising Isaac?

3. What would this story tell Moses about the nature of God?

4. What can we glean about God's nature in this story for our present-day lives as Christians?

5. How can we learn and keep God's charge, statutes, commandments, and laws?

SESSION 11 | SMALL GROUP: 3 (JACOB)

I AM GOD THE ANCIENT ONE

A. Read the following verses.

Genesis 28:10-22

"Now Jacob went out from Beersheba and went toward Haran. So he came to a certain place and stayed there all night, because the sun had set. And he took one of the stones of that place and put it at his head, and he lay down in that place to sleep. Then he dreamed, and behold, a ladder was set up on the earth, and its top reached to heaven; and there the angels of God were ascending and descending on it.

And behold, the LORD stood above it and said: 'I am the LORD God of Abraham your father and the God of Isaac; the land on which you lie I will give to you and your descendants. Also your descendants shall be as the dust of the earth; you shall spread abroad to the west and the east, to the north and the south; and in you and in your seed all the families of the earth shall be blessed. Behold, I am with you and will keep you wherever you go, and will bring you back to this land; for I will not leave you until I have done what I have spoken to you.'

Then Jacob awoke from his sleep and said, 'Surely the LORD is in this place, and I did not know it.' And he was afraid and said, 'How awesome is this place! This is none other than the house of God, and this is the gate of heaven!' Then Jacob rose early in the morning, and took the stone that he had put at his head, set it up as a pillar, and poured oil on top of it. And he called the name of that place Bethel; but the name of that city had been Luz previously. Then Jacob made a vow, saying, 'If God will be with me, and keep me in this way that I am going, and give me bread to eat and clothing to put on, so that I come back to my father's house in peace, then the LORD shall be my God. And this stone which I have set as a pillar shall be God's house, and of all that You give me I will surely give a tenth to You.'"

B. Discuss and answer the following questions.

1. What does Jacob's response to God teach us about obedience?

2. What was God promising Jacob?

3. What would this story tell Moses about the Israelites' life in Egypt?

4. What can we glean about God's nature in this story for our present-day lives as Christians?

I AM GOD THE ANCIENT ONE

Genesis 1:2
"The earth was without form, and void; and darkness was on the face of the deep. And the Spirit of God was hovering over the face of the waters."

Psalm 20:7, NASB
"Some boast in chariots, and some in horses; but we will boast in the name of the Lord, our God."

Acts 20:35
"It is more blessed to give than to receive."

God the Warrior

WHAT YOU NEED

WHAT YOU NEED

- One copy of the curriculum for the teacher
- Bibles
- One copy of the Quotes and Verses handout for each student
- Pens or pencils for each student
- Enough copies of the worksheet for everyone

RECOMMENDED READING

Teachers would greatly benefit from reading John Paul Jackson's two books *I AM: 365 Names of God* and *I AM: Inheriting the Fullness of God's Name*, both available from Streams Ministries (www.streamsministries.com or 1.888.441.8080). *I AM: 365 Names of God* is also available on a worship/meditation CD from Streams.

MULTIMEDIA IDEAS

POWERPOINT

Do a Google (http://images.google.com) image search for the word *Warrior*. Put some of the pictures together in a looping presentation.

VIDEO

The animated film *The Prince of Egypt* includes a fantastic scene of the Israelites crossing the Red Sea. God sends a wall of fire to hold the Egyptians off while Moses parts the sea. Very powerful and worth watching.

INTERNET

A number of Winston Churchill's World War II speeches are available on the British Broadcasting Corporation's (BBC) website at http://www.bbc.co.uk - history/war/wwtwo/churchill_audio.shtml.

The BBC has several fantastic war animations that could be used, all listed at http://www.bbc.co.uk/history/multimedia_zone/animations/. Our suggestion is to show an animation while playing the song below.

SONGS

Chris Janzen's "Raise It Up" is an anthem of worship to God. It can be found on the album *W2* from Friends Langley Vineyard, available from Streams Ministries (www.streamsministries.com or 1.888.441.8080).

God the Warrior

INTRODUCTION

Through the centuries Christians' views of God have changed radically.

——>> **When you think of Jesus, what images come to your mind?**

Lots of people think of Jesus as being meek and mild. They picture Him in a pretty white robe, with a dazzling blue sash, and a halo glowing around His head. On His face is a slight smile. His eyes always look on the verge of tears. Jesus is the Prince of Peace, but we have developed an image of Him as being almost a wuss.

Nothing could be further from the truth! Jesus was strong and courageous. He took on the ruling authorities of His day, starting a revolution. In fact, He was a warrior. Listen to this description of Him [*Have a student read Exodus 15:3; it's on the Quotes and Verses handout*]: "The LORD is a man of war; the LORD is His name."

It's a paradox that a Man who is called the Prince of Peace could also be a Man of War! Our human minds can't figure it out. It's not like the mild-mannered Clark Kent who steps into a phone booth and becomes the powerful Superman: always one or the other. God is both peaceful and warlike at the same time! He is fully the Prince of Peace and fully the Man of War, all the time. The apostle Paul mentioned this fact in Romans 16:20 [*Have a student read Romans 16:20; it's on the Quotes and Verses handout*]: "The God of peace will soon crush Satan under your feet."

——>> **How do you think God handles being a Man of War and a Prince of Peace at the same time?**

THE IMPORTANCE OF GOD'S NAMES

To be truly great, a warrior needs to understand the idea of authority. If we are marked by the name of the Lord, we will carry His authority. As a Christian whose life reflects the character of Jesus, we are able to have His authority. The source of authority is not just in the name of God itself, but in the character it stands for. If we are marked by the name of the Lord, then we will also be marked by the character and the authority of Jesus.

Because we are powerful, it is easy to become arrogant and uncaring in how we wield that power. But God constantly reminds us, through the example of the life of Jesus, that it is humility that marks a great warrior. The apostle James wrote that God resists the proud but gives grace to the humble. Jesus was the ultimate servant; the gospels say that He was meek and lowly of heart.

Those who are marked by the name of God are those who have embraced the value of humility and have discovered the mystery of God's grace.

——>> What do you think grace is?

Grace is the supernatural gift of God to help us be what we are not and to do what we cannot. Those who are humble shall be great in the Kingdom because they have learned to keep themselves within the scope of God's work. They have learned to deny themselves in order to more fully serve Christ. Jesus Himself spoke of the value of the humble in His Sermon on the Mount [*Have a student read Matthew 5:3; it's on the Quotes and Verses handout*]: "Blessed are the poor in spirit, for theirs is the kingdom of heaven."

——>> What does Jesus mean by the phrase *poor in spirit*?

One of the greatest dangers in the Kingdom of God is the sin of spiritual pride. But those who wear the mark of humility have a shield of protection against this evil. These people no longer worry about having to prove anything to anyone—they are totally secure in the Father's love and acceptance. They bear the mark of humility because they bear the name of God.

——>> What do you think humility is?

Humility includes four qualities: 1) being accountable to those we trust, 2) knowing our identity is rooted in God's love, 3) serving others, 4) and being quick to forgive.

——>> Which of these qualities do you think is the most difficult: trusting, knowing God's love, serving, or forgiving?

God's name is at stake in us. People will see God through the way we represent Him. Non-Christians don't read their Bibles to discover God—they read their Christian friends and family. They read us!

Last time we read a verse that David wrote, and it bears repeating here [*Have a student read Psalm 20:7, NASB; it's on the Quotes and Verses handout*]: "Some boast in chariots, and some in horses; but we will boast in the name of the Lord, our God." In Hebrew the phrase *to boast in* means "to have confidence in, to trust in." Boasting in God's name indicates that we have confidence in His character, His attributes, His nature—who He is. God longs to free us from the sinful way we doubt and try to take care of ourselves. This is the way of the world, but God's way is different.

We can be confident in the love God has for us. The confidence of the world can be shaken because ultimately it is dependent upon human strength. The confidence that God wants to give us never ends; it cannot be disappointed, it cannot falter, it cannot fail, because it is rooted in the very foundation of His presence, character, and nature. It is rooted in the unshakable foundation of His name!

God is extending the fullness of His name to each of us today. He is offering to put His name on us and to give us every blessing that comes with it.

I AM GOD THE WARRIOR WORKSHEET

As a warrior, God employs five attributes of His nature: honor, courage, perseverance, loyalty, and strategy. We'll talk about each in a few minutes, but first, I'd like to get your take on what these five qualities mean.

On your worksheets are five qualities God possesses. Under each one write a brief description of what you think that quality means, and a situation in your life where you could use that aspect of His nature. [*Encourage the students to work together . . . give them as long as they need to go through the sheet.*]

SESSION 12—WORKSHEET
I AM GOD THE WARRIOR

God, the mightiest of all warriors, encapsulates all that is good and noble. Because of His purity and grace, His ways are above question. He is a God of peace and of war and holds the tension of those seemingly opposite ideas in perfect balance.

Below are five qualities God possesses. Under each one write a brief description of what you think that quality means, and a situation in your life where you could use that aspect of His nature.

What is **HONOR?** _____

Where could it be applied in your life? _____

_____

What is **COURAGE?** _____

Where could it be applied in your life? _____

_____

What is **PERSEVERANCE?** _____

Where could it be applied in your life? _____

_____

What is **LOYALTY?** _____

Where could it be applied in your life? _____

_____

What is **STRATEGY?** _____

Where could it be applied in your life? _____

_____

I AM GOD THE WARRIOR

God may be a warrior, but He isn't violent for the sake of violence. His heart is full of compassion and grace. He loves us, and sometimes that love has to be protected from an enemy who is desperate to destroy it.

God the Warrior always deals with us in five trustworthy ways: with honor, courage, perseverance, loyalty, and strategy. This is who He is. He cannot help but be this way with us. It's a non-negotiable piece of His nature.

The first attribute God possesses is honor.

——>> What do you think honor is?

A warrior's honor is their most important possession. Honor is about acting in a way that is worthy of respect. Doing what you say you will do. Jesus always acted honorably. He treated others with deep respect and love. Judas Iscariot, the disciple who betrayed Him, was always treated equally as well as the other disciples.

Honor is about being righteous. In Psalm 23:3, we read of how God leads us into battle [*Have a student read Psalm 23:3; it's on the Quotes and Verses handout*]: "He restores my soul; He leads me in the paths of righteousness for His name's sake." To be worthy of the kind of honor God carries, we must rely on Him to protect and lead us, as we read in Psalm 7:10 [*Have a student read Psalm 7:10; it's on the Quotes and Verses handout*]: "My defense is of God, who saves the upright in heart."

——>> How can your life count for something?

The second aspect of God's warrior nature is courage.

——>> What do you think courage is?

Jesus showed incredible courage in how He dealt with those who opposed Him. He never shrunk back from a challenge. Even though He knew He would be murdered for His ministry, He didn't blink. The author Ernest Hemingway once said that courage was "grace under pressure." That description certainly fits Jesus' life.

——>> Do you show grace under pressure?

Courage is a vital ingredient for any great warrior. Throughout history men and women have taken risks and won almost unimaginable victories. God wants His children to be full of courage, knowing that they have a great Father protecting and loving them.

The third aspect of God's warrior nature is perseverance.

——>> What do you think perseverance is?

Perseverance is about holding on, no matter what. There is a famous story about Winston Churchill, the former prime minister of England. In 1941, with his country barely holding on under the attack of Nazi Germany, Churchill made a speech at his former high school. The hall was packed to hear the prime minister's words. What would he say? What would he tell the next generation of English men and women? Could he bring hope in the middle of England's most hopeless time?

Churchill went to the podium and said just three words. "Never give up!" he said, and then went and sat back down. No one moved. Churchill got up a second time, went to the podium, and yelled, "Never give up!" Again he sat back down. This time some scattered applause erupted. Finally Churchill stood up a third time and came to the podium. "Never give up!" he shouted at the top of his lungs. The crowd cheered and cheered. The speech—all nine words of it—would become legendary.

Perseverance is about never giving up. In Psalm 121:4, we see how God perseveres [*Have a student read Psalm 121:4; it's on the Quotes and Verses handout*]: "Behold, He who keeps Israel shall neither slumber nor sleep."

——>> What sort of situations do people today need to persevere through?

The fourth attribute of God's warrior nature is loyalty.

——>> What do you think loyalty is?

Loyalty is about loving someone non-negotiably. When you make a commitment to someone, never waver from it. God's feelings toward us never change. On our best day He loves us every bit as much as on our worst day. He is loyal to us. His commitment never wavers.

——>> How can you be more loyal?

The fifth attribute of God's warrior nature is strategy.

——>> **What do you think strategy is?**

God is not ruling the world haphazardly. He has a distinct, complete plan. He knows what He wants to accomplish. He has a strategy behind everything He is doing. God is a brilliant general, as we can see in Isaiah 11:2 [*Have a student read Isaiah 11:2; it's on the Quotes and Verses handout*]: "The Spirit of the LORD shall rest upon Him, the Spirit of wisdom and understanding, the Spirit of counsel and might, the Spirit of knowledge and of the fear of the LORD."

God has a strategic plan for your life that is greater than you could ever dream. Everything that happens around you happens with one purpose in mind: to make you and God closer. He wants to share everything with each of you. This is His strategy.

——>> **Have you ever seen God's strategy come to completion in an unlikely situation?**

——>> **What do you think God dreams about you?**

CONCLUSION

[*Pray that God would reveal more of His character to each of the students. Thank Him for His mighty name. You may want to close with the Lord's Prayer, which is on the Quotes and Verses handout.*]

I AM GOD THE WARRIOR

God, the mightiest of all warriors, encapsulates all that is good and noble. Because of His purity and grace, His ways are above question. He is a God of peace and of war, and holds the tension of those seemingly opposite ideas in perfect balance.

Below are five qualities God possesses. Under each one, write a brief description of what you think that quality means and a situation in your life where you could use that aspect of His nature.

What is HONOR? _____

Where could it be applied in your life? _____

_____

What is COURAGE? _____

Where could it be applied in your life? _____

_____

What is PERSEVERANCE?_____

Where could it be applied in your life? _____

_____

What is LOYALTY? _____

Where could it be applied in your life? _____

_____

What is STRATEGY?_____

Where could it be applied in your life? _____

_____

I AM GOD THE WARRIOR

Exodus 15:3
"The LORD is a man of war; the LORD is His name."

Romans 16:20, NIV
"The God of peace will soon crush Satan under your feet."

Matthew 5:3
"Blessed are the poor in spirit, for theirs is the kingdom of heaven."

Psalm 20:7, NASB
"Some boast in chariots, and some in horses; but we will boast in the name of the Lord, our God."

Psalm 23:3
"He restores my soul; He leads me in the paths of righteousness for His name's sake."

Psalm 7:10
"My defense is of God, who saves the upright in heart."

Psalm 121:4
"Behold, He who keeps Israel shall neither slumber nor sleep."

Isaiah 11:2
"The Spirit of the LORD shall rest upon Him, the Spirit of wisdom and understanding, the Spirit of counsel and might, the Spirit of knowledge and of the fear of the LORD."

Lord's Prayer (Matthew 6:9–13)
Our Father in heaven,
Hallowed be Your name.
Your kingdom come.
Your will be done
On earth as it is in heaven.
Give us this day our daily bread.
And forgive us our debts,
As we forgive our debtors.
And do not lead us into temptation,
But deliver us from the evil one.
For Yours is the kingdom and the power and the glory forever. Amen.

ABOUT THE AUTHORS

An internationally known speaker and author, **John Paul Jackson** has served for more than a quarter of a century as an advisor, mentor, teacher, pastor, and friend to leaders and students around the world. Founder of Streams Ministries International, Streams Institute for Spiritual Development, Streams Publishing House, and Streams Music Group, John Paul is a highly sought after teacher and conference speaker. He has authored several books, developed curricula, produced multiple worship recordings, and appeared on numerous television broadcasts. John Paul and his wife, Diane, have two sons and three grandchildren and live in the Dartmouth/Lake Sunapee region of New Hampshire.

A trained journalist, **Jordan Bateman** worked for six years as a reporter for *The Langley Advance News*. During his time at the paper, he worked to help a number of valuable causes, including the move toward palliative care in medicine, autistic children's issues, and child literacy. In September 2002, he left the paper to launch his own small business, Outlawed Wonderings Media Group, a freelance writing and editing firm. He is director of Next Generation Ministries at Friends Langley Vineyard Church, overseeing the church's work with babies, children, teenagers, and young adults. In addition he facilitates The Well, a network of youth ministries from across the Greater Vancouver area. Jordan's wife, Jennifer, is a youth pastor at Friends Langley Vineyard, and they live in Langley, British Columbia with their daughter, Indiana Glory.

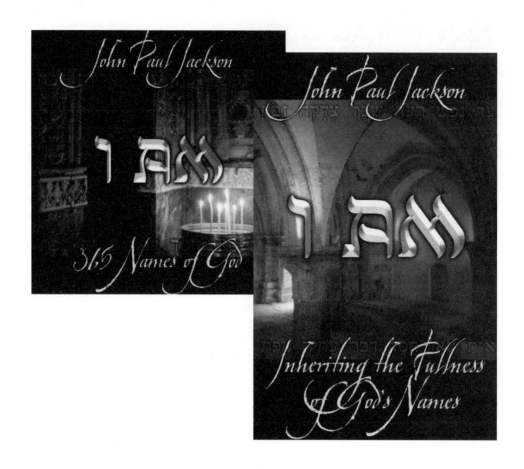

I AM: 365 NAMES OF GOD

Designed for daily reading and meditation, John Paul Jackson
has collected 365 names of God that will guide you into
becoming a person who consistently abides in God's presence.
Hardback.

RETAIL $24

I AM: INHERITING THE FULLNESS OF GOD'S NAMES

As you embark on the glorious adventure of knowing God, let
Him show you the amazing mysteries and wonders revealed for
those who bear His name.

RETAIL $10

I AM: 365 NAMES OF GOD CD

Listen as John Paul Jackson reads the names of God from his book. Experience the peace, comfort, healing, provision, and transforming power that comes from meditating on God's names.

RETAIL $16

BREATH OF I AM CD

Ideal for times of meditation, prayer, and therapeutic healing, this soothing instrumental creates an atmosphere that will soothe your spirit and calm your soul.

RETAIL $16

NEEDLESS CASUALTIES OF WAR

Unlock the secrets of effective spiritual warfare. Discover foundational truths that will help you fight with wisdom and authority. John Paul Jackson offers a theology of spiritual warfare that is so simple, yet so profound. Foreword by John Sandford.

RETAIL $13

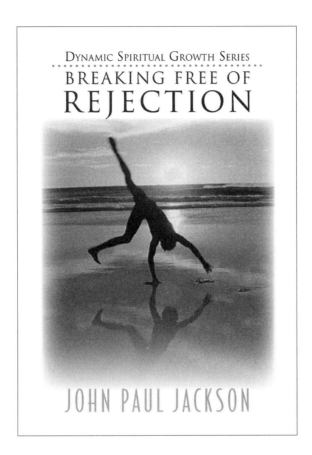

BREAKING FREE OF REJECTION

In this compassionate and spiritually insightful book, John Paul Jackson explains what happens when rejection rules our lives. Discover how to harness the power of rejection, dramatically improve your life, and walk into the extraordinary quality of life God desires for you.

RETAIL $11

UNDERSTANDING DREAMS AND VISIONS

Explore the world of dreams. Unravel the mysteries of dream interpretation in this inspiring series and discover how to apply God-given insights in your waking life. You don't want to miss these fascinating insights from a gifted dream expert.

(Six-CD set)

RETAIL $42

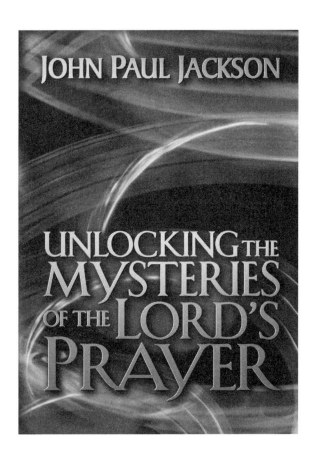

UNLOCKING THE MYSTERIES OF THE LORD'S PRAYER

Are you hungry for a deeper revelation of prayer? Uncover seven dimensions of the Lord's prayer and grasp essential keys that open the doors of Heaven.

(Four-CD set)

RETAIL $27

STREAMS INSTITUTE FOR SPIRITUAL DEVELOPMENT

JOHN PAUL JACKSON, FOUNDER

At Streams, we seek to give shape to ideas that educate, inform, and cause people to better understand and delight in God. We endeavor to enrich people's lives by satisfying their lifelong need to identify and use their God-given gifts. We seek to be used by God to heal, renew, and encourage pastors and church leaders.

COURSES OFFERED INCLUDE:

Course 101: The Art of Hearing God
Course 102: Advanced Prophetic Ministry
Course 104: Reaching Your Destiny in God
Course 201: Understanding Dreams and Visions
Course 202: Advanced Workshop in Dream Interpretation

**More information is available online at
www.streamsministries.com or by calling 1.888.441.8080**

ORDER FORM

🖱 ORDER ONLINE: **www.streamsministries.com**

☎ CALL TOLL-FREE (U.S. AND CANADA): **1.888.441.8080**

📪 POSTAL ORDERS: **Streams Ministries, P.O. Box 550, North Sutton, NH 03260 USA**

QUANTITY	TITLE	PRICE
_____	_____	_____
_____	_____	_____
_____	_____	_____
_____	_____	_____

DOMESTIC SHIPPING AND HANDLING CHARGES   SUBTOTAL _____

Up to $20	$5.00
$20.01 to $50.00	$7.00
$50.01 to $75.00	$8.00
$75.01 to $100.00	$9.00
More than $100	10% of Subtotal

SHIPPING AND HANDLING _____

TOTAL THIS ORDER _____

For AK, HI, PR, USVI, Canada, or Mexico, please double the shipping charges.

INTERNATIONAL RATES: All international orders must be paid by credit card only. Please specify international surface or airmail shipping. The shipping cost will be added to your credit card charges.
(PLEASE PRINT CLEARLY)

NAME: _____

STREET ADDRESS: _____

APT._____ **CITY:** _____

STATE:_____ **ZIP:**_____ **COUNTRY:** _____

PHONE: _____

E-MAIL: _____

METHOD OF PAYMENT:
___ Check or Money Order (Make check payable to Streams Ministries)
___ Credit Card: ❑ Visa ❑ MasterCard ❑ American Express ❑ Discover

CARD NUMBER: _____-_____-_____-_____ EXPIRATION DATE:___/____

CARD HOLDER (please print): _____

SIGNATURE: _____
(Credit card orders cannot be processed without signature)